ADMITTING SYRIAN REFUGEES: THE INTELLIGENCE VOID AND THE EMERGING HOMELAND SECURITY THREAT

HEARING

BEFORE THE

SUBCOMMITTEE ON COUNTERTERRORISM AND INTELLIGENCE

OF THE

COMMITTEE ON HOMELAND SECURITY HOUSE OF REPRESENTATIVES

ONE HUNDRED FOURTEENTH CONGRESS

FIRST SESSION

JUNE 24, 2015

Serial No. 114–22

Printed for the use of the Committee on Homeland Security

Available via the World Wide Web: http://www.gpo.gov/fdsys/

U.S. GOVERNMENT PUBLISHING OFFICE

96–168 PDF   WASHINGTON : 2015

For sale by the Superintendent of Documents, U.S. Government Publishing Office
Internet: bookstore.gpo.gov   Phone: toll free (866) 512–1800; DC area (202) 512–1800
Fax: (202) 512–2104   Mail: Stop IDCC, Washington, DC 20402–0001

COMMITTEE ON HOMELAND SECURITY

MICHAEL T. MCCAUL, Texas, *Chairman*

LAMAR SMITH, Texas
PETER T. KING, New York
MIKE ROGERS, Alabama
CANDICE S. MILLER, Michigan, *Vice Chair*
JEFF DUNCAN, South Carolina
TOM MARINO, Pennsylvania
LOU BARLETTA, Pennsylvania
SCOTT PERRY, Pennsylvania
CURT CLAWSON, Florida
JOHN KATKO, New York
WILL HURD, Texas
EARL L. "BUDDY" CARTER, Georgia
MARK WALKER, North Carolina
BARRY LOUDERMILK, Georgia
MARTHA MCSALLY, Arizona
JOHN RATCLIFFE, Texas
DANIEL M. DONOVAN, JR., New York

BENNIE G. THOMPSON, Mississippi
LORETTA SANCHEZ, California
SHEILA JACKSON LEE, Texas
JAMES R. LANGEVIN, Rhode Island
BRIAN HIGGINS, New York
CEDRIC L. RICHMOND, Louisiana
WILLIAM R. KEATING, Massachusetts
DONALD M. PAYNE, JR., New Jersey
FILEMON VELA, Texas
BONNIE WATSON COLEMAN, New Jersey
KATHLEEN M. RICE, New York
NORMA J. TORRES, California

BRENDAN P. SHIELDS, *Staff Director*
JOAN V. O'HARA, *General Counsel*
MICHAEL S. TWINCHEK, *Chief Clerk*
I. LANIER AVANT, *Minority Staff Director*

————

SUBCOMMITTEE ON COUNTERTERRORISM AND INTELLIGENCE

PETER T. KING, New York, *Chairman*

CANDICE S. MILLER, Michigan
LOU BARLETTA, Pennsylvania
JOHN KATKO, New York
WILL HURD, Texas
MICHAEL T. MCCAUL, Texas *(ex officio)*

BRIAN HIGGINS, New York
WILLIAM R. KEATING, Massachusetts
FILEMON VELA, Texas
BENNIE G. THOMPSON, Mississippi *(ex officio)*

MANDY BOWERS, *Subcommittee Staff Director*
DENNIS TERRY, *Subcommittee Clerk*
HOPE GOINS, *Minority Subcommittee Staff Director*

(II)

CONTENTS

ADMITTING SYRIAN REFUGEES: THE INTELLIGENCE VOID AND THE EMERGING HOMELAND SECURITY THREAT

Wednesday, June 24, 2015

U.S. HOUSE OF REPRESENTATIVES,
COMMITTEE ON HOMELAND SECURITY,
SUBCOMMITTEE ON COUNTERTERRORISM AND INTELLIGENCE,
Washington, DC.

The subcommittee met, pursuant to call, at 10:07 a.m., in Room 311, Cannon House Office Building, Hon. Peter T. King [Chairman of the subcommittee] presiding.

Present: Representatives King, Barletta, Katko, McCaul, Higgins, Keating, Vela, and Thompson.

Mr. KING. Good morning. The Committee on Homeland Security Subcommittee on Counterterrorism and Intelligence will come to order. We are waiting for the Ranking Member, who has been detained. He has graciously said we could start the hearing without him. He will be coming shortly, as will, I believe, the Chairman of the full committee.

So, the subcommittee is meeting today to hear testimony from three distinguished experts regarding the security situation in Iraq and Syria and to review potential vulnerabilities in the refugee screening process. I would like to welcome the Members of the subcommittee and express my appreciation to the witnesses who are here today. Now I will make an opening statement.

For Americans opening our doors to those who flee violence or exploitation, this is part of who we are as a Nation. America has a long and proud history of providing safe harbor to refugees. Refugees admitted to America include our former colleague, the late Congressman Tom Lantos from Hungary, scientist Albert Einstein from Germany, among thousands more who have contributed to American society. But we have also had refugees and asylum seekers who take advantage of U.S. safe haven to plot and carry out attacks.

Over the last 4 years, the conflict in Syria has forced more than 3.9 million Syrians to flee their country, in large part due to the continued violence and savagery of ISIS, making this one of the world's biggest refugee crises without an end in sight. This year, the United States is expected to admit several thousand Syrian refugees, a number only expected to rise over the next few years, as well as almost 70,000 refugees from approximately 70 countries.

We have heard open and closed testimony from Government officials and security experts expressing concerns that terrorist groups may seek to use Syrian refugee programs as a gateway to carry out attacks in Europe and America. It is essential that we have a discussion of the humanitarian crises and the security risks inherent in the process. I agree that the vast majority of Syrian refugees do not have ties to terror groups. However, we have been reviewing the current security vetting procedures for a number of months. I have a number of concerns, not the least of which is the lack of on-the-ground intelligence necessary to identify terror links.

With the lack of stable foreign governments, foreign intelligence agencies, military intelligence, U.S. Embassies abroad, and access to human intelligence on the ground in Syria, the information and intelligence that we are able to acquire regarding individuals who seek to enter the United States is limited and oftentimes unverifiable. This significantly degrades the quality and accuracy of our vetting process.

The United States has seen the danger of flawed refugee vetting, as well as the potential for refugees to be radicalized once they are in the United States. In 2011, I held a hearing on Islamic radicalization within the Somali-American community. This included the 20-plus cases of individuals, many refugees or children of refugees, who left the United States to join al-Shabaab. Since that time, we have seen about a dozen other Somali-American youths join ISIS.

On May 25, 2011, two Iraqi refugees were arrested in Bowling Green, Kentucky and charged with conspiracy to kill U.S. nationals abroad, attempting to provide material support to terrorists and to al-Qaeda in Iraq, and 21 other charges. According to a July 2011 news article, the FBI was looking into potential terror ties for approximately 300 additional Iraqi refugees. Other cases include the blind sheik, Omar Abdel Rahman, the 1993 World Trade Bomber Ramzi Yousef, Mir Qazi involved in the 1997 CIA headquarters shooting, and, of course, the Tsarnaev brothers in Boston. While these bad actors represent a small percentage of the total number of refugees in the United States, we have to continuously monitor the changing threat environments.

In just the past 3 weeks, there have been at least 10 arrests by the FBI of U.S. individuals connected with ISIS and plotting attacks on the homeland. The on-line radicalization and calls by ISIS leadership for Islamists to carry out attacks in the United States are resonating with small pockets of U.S. society. There is little doubt that these calls for attacks are also resonating within the refugee community both domestically and those still abroad. This does not mean we should close our borders and not accept anyone. But we certainly need to be thoughtful and deliberative about the process and provide the American people with the most assurance that we are not importing terrorists.

There is no doubt that a number of significant improvements were made to the refugee vetting process in 2011 after the alarming cases involving the Iraqi refugees. At the same time, there have been procedural failures that resulted in denial of refugee status for a number of Iraqi and Afghani nationals who put their lives on the line to help the United States during the military campaigns.

We have invited a distinguished panel of experts testifying today to assess the current threat environment, to share their perspectives on refugee vetting, and to solicit their recommendations on what additional security measures should be considered.

[The statement of Chairman King follows:]

STATEMENT OF CHAIRMAN PETER T. KING

For Americans, opening our doors to those who flee violence, war, and exploitation is part of who we are as a Nation. America has a long and proud history of providing safe harbor for refugees. Refugees admitted to America include Congressman Tom Lantos (Hungary) and scientist Albert Einstein (Germany), among thousands more who have contributed to U.S society. But we have also had refugees and asylum seekers take advantage of U.S. safe haven to plot and carry out attacks.

Over the last 4 years, the conflict in Syria has forced more than 3.9 million Syrians to flee their country, in large part due to the continued violence and savagery of ISIS, making this one of the world's biggest refugee crises without an end in sight. This year, the United States is expected to admit several thousand Syrian refugees—a number only expected to rise over the next few years as well as almost 70,000 refugees from approximately 70 countries.

We have heard open and closed testimony from Government officials and security experts expressing concerns that terrorist groups may seek to use Syrian refugee programs as a gateway to carry out attacks in Europe and America. It is essential that we have a discussion of the humanitarian crisis and the security risks inherent in the process.

I agree that the vast majority of Syrian refugees do not have ties to terror groups. However, we have been reviewing the current security vetting procedures for a number of months, and I have a number of concerns, not the least of which is the lack of on-the-ground intelligence necessary to identify terror links.

With the lack of stable foreign governments, foreign intelligence agencies, military intelligence, U.S. embassy support, and access to human intelligence on the ground in Syria, the information and intelligence that we are able to acquire regarding individuals who seek to enter the United States is limited, and oftentimes unverifiable. This significantly degrades the quality and accuracy of our vetting process.

The United States has seen the danger of flawed refugee vetting, as well as the potential for refugees to be radicalized once they are in the United States.

In 2011, I held a hearing into Islamist radicalization within the Somali-American community. This included the 20-plus cases of individuals, many refugees or children of refugees, who left the United States to join al-Shabaab. Since that time, we have seen about a dozen other Somali-American youth join ISIS.

On May 25, 2011, two Iraqi refugees were arrested in Bowling Green, Kentucky and charged with conspiracy to kill U.S. nationals abroad; attempting to provide material support to terrorists and to al-Qaeda in Iraq; and 21 other charges. According to a July 2011 news article *(LA Times)*, the FBI was looking into potential terror ties for approximately 300 additional Iraqi refugees.

Other cases include the Blind Sheikh—Omar Abdel Rahman, 1993 World Trade Center bomber Ramzi Yousef, Mir Aimal Kansi the 1997 CIA Headquarters shooter, and the Tsarnaev brothers.

While these bad actors represent only a small percentage of the total number of refugees in the United States, we have to continuously monitor the changing threat environment. In just the past 3 weeks, there have been at least 10 arrests by the FBI of U.S. individuals connected with ISIS and plotting attacks in the homeland.

The on-line radicalization and calls by ISIS leadership for Islamists to carry out attacks in the United States are resonating with small pockets of U.S. society. There is little doubt that these calls for attacks are also resonating within the refugee community—both domestically and those still abroad. This doesn't mean that we should close our borders and not accept anyone, but we certainly need to be thoughtful and deliberative about the process and provide the American people with the most assurance that we are not importing terrorists.

There is no doubt that a number of significant improvements were made to the refugee vetting process in 2011, after the alarming cases involving several Iraqi refugees. At the same time, there has been procedural failures that resulted in the denial of refugee status for a number of Iraqi and Afghani nationals who put their lives on the line to help the United States during the military campaigns.

We have invited a distinguished panel of experts testifying today to assess the current threat environment, share their perspectives on refugee vetting and solicit their recommendations on what additional security measures should be considered.

Mr. KING. Now I recognize the Ranking Member of the full committee, the gentleman from Mississippi, Mr. Thompson, for an opening statement.

Mr. THOMPSON. Thank you very much, Mr. Chairman. It is good to see you. Let me welcome the witnesses to the hearing. I appreciate you holding this hearing.

It is important for us in looking at the United States refugee program and see how it was impacted by the terrorist attacks of September 11. In the aftermath of those attacks, a review of refugee-related security procedures were undertaken. Refugee admissions were briefly suspended. Enhanced security measures were implemented. However, more than a decade after the enhanced security measures have been undertaken, with limited instances of fraud, there are those who believe that certain populations are unable to be properly vetted for security purposes.

Rather than focus on the fear and concern surrounding Syrian refugees, I think we should focus on the known facts about the Syrian refugee population. The Syrian people are the primary victims of the violent conflict in Syria and the brutal actions of ISIL. They are the most vulnerable to the violence, and have known first-hand the cruelty of ISIL and other groups that have brought harm upon their communities. These refugees, like most others that arrive in the United States, are fleeing difficult, even life-threatening situations. The idea that they would be met with suspicion and hate upon arrival in the United States is an affront to the values we uphold and promote.

Like Americans, most Syrians consider ISIL to be their enemy as well. Within the United States, the Syrian American Council has already partnered with the Office of Civil Rights and Civil Liberties within the Department of Homeland Security to organize community briefings for Syrian Americans focused on countering violent extremism. Groups like this encourage a robust Congressional debate on how ISIL can be stopped both at home and abroad. In fact, the leading demographic of those seeking or joining ISIL is in the United States who were born U.S. citizens, including citizens with no ancestry from major Muslim countries. Therefore, preventing vulnerable Syrian refugees from entering the United States will not address the Unites States issue with violent extremism.

Time and time again, I have urged this committee not to have a narrow view of violent extremism which ignores violent extremist activities of domestic groups. Regrettably, last week's attack at the Emanuel AME Church in Charleston brought this issue into stark focus. Congress, the President, and the Department of Homeland Security need to come together with the State and local governments to honestly acknowledge that domestic terrorism is a threat to the safety and security of the American homeland, including the refugees who resettle within our borders.

We must move beyond the perceived fears of the unknown and focus on credible threat information and allow the security vetting systems we have in place to work. I yield back, Mr. Chairman.

[The statement of Ranking Member Thompson follows:]

STATEMENT OF RANKING MEMBER BENNIE G. THOMPSON

JUNE 24, 2015

Mr. Chairman, I would like to thank you for holding this hearing to examine the United States' security screening process of Syrian refugees and the threats those refugees may pose to the United States.

The United States refugee program was greatly impacted by the terrorist attacks of September 11. In the aftermath of those attacks, a review of refugee-related security procedures was undertaken, refugee admissions were briefly suspended, and enhanced security measures were implemented.

However, more than a decade after these enhanced security measures have been undertaken with limited instances of fraud, there are those that believe certain populations are unable to be properly vetted for security purposes. Rather than focus on the fear and concern surrounding Syrian refugees, I think we should focus on the known facts about the Syrian refugee population. The Syrian people are the primary victims of the violent conflict in Syria and the brutal actions of ISIL.

They are the most vulnerable to the violence and know first-hand the cruelty of ISIL and other groups that have brought harm upon their communities. These refugees, like most others that arrive in the United States, are fleeing difficult, even life-threatening, situations. The idea that they would be met with suspicion and hate upon arrival in the United States is an affront to the values we uphold and promote.

Like Americans, most Syrians consider ISIL to be their enemy, as well. Within the United States, the Syrian American Council has already partnered with the Office for Civil Rights and Civil Liberties within the Department of Homeland Security to organize community briefings for Syrian Americans focused on countering violent extremism. Groups like this encourage a robust Congressional debate on how ISIL can be stopped both at home and abroad.

In fact, the leading demographic of those seeking or joining ISIL in the United States are U.S.-born citizens, including citizens with no ancestry from majority-Muslim countries. Therefore, preventing vulnerable Syrian refugees from entering the United States will not address the United States' issues with violent extremism.

Time and time again, I have urged this committee not to have a narrow view of violent extremism, which ignores violent extremist activity of domestic groups. Regrettably, last week's attacks at the Emanuel AME Church in Charleston brought this issue into stark focus. Congress, the President, and the Department of Homeland Security need to come together with State and local governments to honestly acknowledge that domestic terrorism is a threat to the safety and security of the American homeland, including the refugees who resettle within our borders.

We must move beyond the perceived fears of the unknown and focus on credible threat information and allow the security vetting systems we have in place to work. I yield back.

Mr. KING. The Ranking Member yields back.

I recognize the Chairman of the full committee, the gentleman from Texas, Mr. McCaul.

Mr. MCCAUL. Thank you, Mr. Chairman. I want to thank you for holding this important hearing. We have been sounding the alarm for months on this issue and for good reason. America has a proud tradition of welcoming refugees and immigrants. But we need to make sure the extremists do not exploit this pathway to our country, especially from terrorist safe havens.

Last year, the administration announced plans to surge the admission of Syrian refugees into the United States, including plans to resettle roughly 2,000 of them this year and thousands more next year. This is concerning for two reasons. First, terrorists have made it known that they want to manipulate refugee programs to sneak operatives into the West. Second, top National security officials have admitted that intelligence gaps in Syria will make it hard to weed them out of refugee pools.

Testifying before our committee in February, the director of the National Counterterrorism Center called these refugees a population of concern given the expansive presence of ISIS and al-

Qaeda in Syria. At the same hearing, the FBI's assistant director, Michael Steinbach, for counterterrorism, argued that identifying potential operatives would be difficult because, ''our databases won't have the information we need.'' Simply put, we cannot screen applicants confidentially if we don't have good intelligence on the ground. We can't vet them properly if we don't have the proper databases.

In light of these concerns, I sent a series of letters to the administration this year highlighting the risk of accelerating Syrian refugee admissions and requesting greater assurances regarding the screening process. The responses were inadequate. The administration was vague in explaining how the screening process would overcome the intelligence gaps. I just wrote the President 2 weeks ago, again, asking for answers and a Classified briefing for Members of this committee. We are still waiting for a serious response. I do not take this issue lightly. Terrorists are constantly probing our defenses and would not hesitate to exploit a program meant to save innocent people fleeing from violence for the purpose of attacking our homeland.

I remind you that members of al-Qaeda in Iraq, the predecessor to ISIS, have already managed to sneak in to our country through refugee settlement programs. Two of these terrorists, arrested in 2009, were responsible for killing four Pennsylvania National Guard soldiers in Iraq. Yet they were gained entry and resettled in Bowling Green, Kentucky. That was when we had far better intelligence on the ground in Iraq to vet refugees, where in Syria we are dark.

The situation today in Syria is even more chaotic, making it difficult to get the biometric, biographic, and other information needed to ensure individuals being admitted into our country do not intend to do our people harm. Since its founding, America has welcomed refugees from conflict zones in the darkest corners of the globe. We will not abandon that tradition. It embodies the compassion of our people and represents our deepest values. But we must also not abandon our vigilance. We cannot be naive.

In Syria, we are witnessing the largest convergence of Islamist terrorists in world history. Some of these fanatics want to turn our refugee programs into a Trojan horse to carry out attacks here at home. We cannot allow that to happen. I hope the White House will do more to convince Congress and the American people that it is moving forward cautiously, appropriately, but most importantly with the security of the American people as a priority. If it does not, we may need to consider taking additional steps here on Capitol Hill. With that, Mr. Chairman, I yield back.

Mr. KING. I thank the Chairman of the full committee for his statement.

Now we will proceed to the witnesses. Other Members of the committee are reminded opening statements may be submitted for the record. We are pleased to have a very distinguished panel of witnesses before us today on this important topic: Dr. Seth Jones, Mr. Tom Fuentes, and Dr. Daveed Gartenstein-Ross.

Beginning with Dr. Jones, he is the associate director of the International Security and Defense Policy Center at the Rand Cooperation, as well as an adjunct professor at Johns Hopkins University School for Advanced International Studies. He served as the representative for the commander of the U.S. Special Operations Commands, the assistant secretary of defense of special operations. Prior to that position, he served as a plans officer and an adviser to the commanding general U.S. Special Ops in Afghanistan.

He specializes in counterinsurgency and counterterrorism, including a focus on Afghanistan, Pakistan, and al-Qaeda. I have been reading all his bio. But the fact is, Dr. Jones has testified before this committee many times. He is a good friend of the committee and he works with us. We appreciate having you back here again today. Dr. Jones, you are recognized for 5 minutes.

STATEMENT OF SETH G. JONES, DIRECTOR, INTERNATIONAL SECURITY AND DEFENSE POLICY CENTER, RAND CORPORATION

Mr. JONES. Thank you, Chairman King. Thank you, Ranking Member Thompson and other distinguished Members of the committee. This is a very important hearing. I will divide my comments into three sections.

The first is an update on the wars in Syria and, to a certain extent, Iraq. The second is to try to tie that back to the homeland. The third is to bring in the refugee issues. Let me start with a brief update. As all of us here know, the wars in both Syria and Iraq, which are deeply intertwined, continue to impact U.S. National security and continue to contribute to large refugee flows. At least by my assessment, in Syria, while the United States is providing limited support to some Syrian rebels through such programs as the Congressionally-approved Train and Equip Program and is conducting some limited air strikes against groups like Daesh and the Khorasan Group, the rest of 2015 is, indeed, concerning.

Daesh or ISIS is likely to remain highly capable in Syria because of its access to resources and its ability to replace killed and captured leaders, as well as to continue to get pretty significant funding streams. In addition, the al-Qaeda-affiliated group, Jabhat al-Nusra in Syria has also increased its control of territory. In fact, at least by my estimates, al-Nusra may be more capable now. By that, I mean more fighters, more funds, and more territory controlled than at any time since its creation in 2011, including in such strongholds as Idlib, Syria.

That brings us to the connection to the homeland. The two groups in Syria, they also operate in Iraq, remain Daesh or ISIS and the Khorasan Group. They present high threats to the U.S. homeland. Both appear to be plotting attacks and certainly trying to inspire attacks in the U.S. homeland, as well as other places in the West. I think the issue that is worth noting is that we have more foreign fighters in this broader battleground that is Syria and Iraq than we have had in any jihadist battlefield in the modern era.

This is a slightly different problem set than what I had to deal with in Afghanistan, what we had to deal with in Libya, and other places. Over 20,000 foreign fighters, about 17 percent or so appear to be coming from the West. Roughly 200 Americans are known to have attempted to travel to Syria to fight with Islamic militants. Obviously, of additional concern is the growing number of attacks we have seen across the West with links either directly or indirectly back to this region.

Garland, Texas, Copenhagen, Denmark in February 2015, Paris, France in January 2015, Sydney, Australia in December 2014, Ottawa, Canada in October 2014, Brussels, Belgium in May 2014, just to name a few. The broader issue, as we look to the ties between Syria and the United States, is, first, more foreign fighters than we have seen on any modern battlefield, and, second, our intelligence picture is clearly much worse than at least my own experience in several battlefields overseas where we had a sustained American presence on the ground to collect information.

So this brings me briefly back to refugees. I am happy to discuss this in more detail. Got roughly 4 million refugees based on the Syria problem set. Refugees has, as the Chairman noted, historically played and will continue to play a critical role in ensuring U.S. economic prosperity and cultural diversity. But the risks associated with refugees may be higher from Syria for several reasons. First, Syria and neighboring Iraq have the highest number of foreign fighters than any modern jihadist battlefield as I have already noted. There has been an exodus of some fighters to the West.

Second, several groups in the region, like Daesh or ISIS, have planned to put operatives in the West, including in Europe, by having them seek political refugee status. This is not just in Syria by the way. We have seen this effort in Libya, among other places. Third, the U.S. intelligence community's understanding of extremists in Syria is worse. I do think it is worth considering a range of issues, improving data management of potentially concerning refugees, rescreening procedures, holding data collected at refugee camps, some DNA checks, and a few other issues.

But let me just say in conclusion, that the United States does have a long-standing tradition of offering protection and freedom to refugees who live in fear of persecution. The Chairman mentioned a number of ones, including Albert Einstein. An integral part of that mission, however, in my view, needs to be ensuring that those refugees considered for entry into the United States, including from such jihadist battlefields as Syria, do not present a risk to the safety and security of the United States. I think what we are looking for is a balance. I am happy to talk more about those specifics in the Q and A period. Thank you, Mr. Chairman.

[The prepared statement of Mr. Jones follows:]

PREPARED STATEMENT OF SETH G. JONES [1][2]

JUNE 24, 2015

Chairman King, Ranking Member Higgins, and distinguished Members of the Subcommittee on Counterterrorism and Intelligence, thank you for inviting me to testify at this important hearing, ''Admitting Syrian Refugees: The Intelligence Void

---

[1] The opinions and conclusions expressed in this testimony are the author's alone and should not be interpreted as representing those of RAND or any of the sponsors of its research. This product is part of the RAND Corporation testimony series. RAND testimonies record testimony presented by RAND associates to Federal, State, or local legislative committees; Government-appointed commissions and panels; and private review and oversight bodies. The RAND Corporation is a non-profit research organization providing objective analysis and effective solutions that address the challenges facing the public and private sectors around the world. RAND's publications do not necessarily reflect the opinions of its research clients and sponsors.

[2] This testimony is available for free download at *http://www.rand.org/pubs/testimonies/CT433.html*.

and the Emerging Home and Security Threat.'' I have divided my comments into four sections. The first provides an overview of the wars in Syria and neighboring Iraq, the second focuses on the terrorism threat to the United States, the third outlines the foreign-fighter problem from Syria and Iraq, and the fourth examines the implications for Syrian refugees.

I. UPDATE ON THE WARS IN SYRIA AND IRAQ

The wars in Syria and Iraq, which are deeply intertwined, continue to impact U.S. National security.

In Syria, the United States is providing limited support to some Syrian rebels against Daesh—also known as the Islamic State of Iraq and the Levant (ISIL), Islamic State of Iraq and al-Sham (ISIS), or simply Islamic State (IS)—under the Congressionally-approved train-and-equip program.[3] However, U.S.-led airstrikes have been insufficient to seriously degrade Daesh in Syria. Over the rest of 2015, Daesh is likely to remain highly capable because of its access to resources and its ability to replace killed and captured leaders. Daesh has recently strengthened control in such Syrian areas as Homs, Dayr az Zawr, and Ar Raqqah. In addition, the al-Qaeda-affiliated Jabhat al-Nusrah has also increased its control of territory. In fact, Jabhat al-Nusrah may be more capable now—with more fighters, funds, and territory—than at any time since its creation in 2011, and it retains a stronghold in northwestern Syrian areas such as Idlib. The recent capture of the town of Jisr al-Shughour in northern Idlib province was just the latest in a string of battlefield victories by rebel forces, which have made advances in both the north and the south of the country.[4]

In neighboring Iraq, the United States is engaged in a counterinsurgency campaign against Daesh and its allies. After nearly 10 months of bombing and U.S. military, intelligence, and diplomatic support to the Iraqi government and local actors, Daesh has lost ground in some areas—including most recently in Tikrit. But Daesh still retains substantial territory in the predominantly Sunni provinces of Anbar, Salaheddine, and Nineveh. In addition, Daesh remains well-funded, allowing it to continue operations. Its funding comes from such activities as smuggling oil, selling stolen goods, kidnapping and extortion, seizing bank accounts, and smuggling antiquities.[5] Daesh's capture of Ramadi in May 2015—despite an intensified U.S. bombing campaign—indicates that the organization retains significant capabilities in some areas.[6]

II. THE TERRORIST THREAT TO THE U.S. HOMELAND

In understanding the threat from Syria and Iraq, it is important to understand the broader context. Not all terrorist groups present a direct threat to the U.S. homeland. As Table 1 highlights, terrorist groups can be divided into three categories: Those that pose a high threat because they are involved in plotting or instigating attacks against the U.S. homeland; those that pose a medium threat because they are involved in plotting attacks against U.S. structures, such as embassies and U.S. citizens overseas (though not against the U.S. homeland); and those that pose a low threat because they are focused on targeting local regimes or other countries.[7] Two terrorist groups operating in Syria—Daesh and the Khorasan Group—present high threats (Table 1).

---

[3] Daesh is an acronym from the Arabic name of the group, al-Dawlah al-Islamiyah fil 'Iraq wal-Sham.

[4] See, for example, Liz Sly, ''Assad's Hold on Power Looks Shakier Than Ever as Rebels Advance in Syria,'' *Washington Post*, April 26, 2015.

[5] See, for example, Patrick B. Johnston, *Countering ISIL's Financing: Testimony Presented Before the House Financial Services Committee on November 13, 2014*, Santa Monica, Calif.: RAND Corporation, CT–419, 2014. On antiquities, see Financial Action Task Force, *Financing of the Terrorist Organization Islamic State in Iraq and the Levant (ISIL)*, Paris: Financial Action Task Force, February 2015.

[6] See, for example, Tim Arango, ''ISIS Captures Key Iraqi City Despite Strikes,'' *New York Times*, May 18, 2015; Hugh Naylor and Mustafa Salim, ''Key City in Iraq Falls to Militants,'' *Washington Post*, May 18, 2015.

[7] Seth G. Jones, *A Persistent Threat: The Evolution of Al Qa'ida and Other Salafi Jihadist*, Santa Monica, Calif.: RAND Corporation, RR–637–OSD, 2014.

TABLE 1.—EXAMPLES OF TERRORISTS THAT THREATEN THE UNITED STATES

	High Threat	Medium Threat	Low Threat
Characteristics	Plotting or instigating attacks against the U.S. homeland and U.S. targets overseas (e.g., U.S. embassies and citizens).	Plotting attacks against U.S. targets overseas (e.g., U.S. embassies and citizens).	Limited or no active plotting against U.S. homeland or U.S. targets overseas.
Examples	• Al Qa'ida in the Arabian Peninsula. • Core al Qa'ida (including the Khorasan Group). • Daesh .... • Some inspired individuals and networks.	• Al Shabaab .... • Jabhat al-Nusrah .... • Ansar al-Sharia Libya groups ...... • Al Qa'ida in the Islamic Maghreb ...... • Boko Haram	• East Turkestan Islamic Movement • Suqor al-Sham

First, some groups pose a high threat. Since its expansion in Iraq and Syria, Daesh has become a growing threat to the United States. Rather than the complex attacks on 9/11, which involved years of training and meticulous planning, the most likely Daesh threat today comes from smaller, less-sophisticated attacks from inspired individuals who may have limited or no connections to the organization. Core al Qa'ida, based in Pakistan, also presents a threat to the U.S. homeland. But their leaders have had difficulty recruiting—or even inspiring—competent operatives in the West. That's why Ayman al-Zawahiri sent a small group of operatives, referred to as the Khorasan Group, to Syria to plot attacks in Europe and the United States. Another is al Qa'ida in the Arabian Peninsula, which provided training to two of the operatives involved in the Charlie Hebdo attacks, Said and Cherif Kouachi. Several Yemen-based operatives—including leader Nasir al-Wuhayshi—continue to plot attacks against the United States. In addition, a small number of inspired individuals, such as the Tsarnaev brothers, who perpetrated the April 2013 Boston Marathon bombings, pose a threat. Still, terrorists have had difficulty striking the U.S. homeland because of robust counterterrorism steps by the Department of Homeland Security, Federal Bureau of Investigation, U.S. intelligence community, and other Federal and local agencies.

Second, several extremist groups pose a medium-level threat because of their interest and capability to target U.S. citizens overseas, though they have little interest or ability to strike the U.S. homeland. Ansar al-Sharia Tunisia, for instance, has planned attacks against U.S. diplomats and infrastructure in Tunis, including the U.S. Embassy. Several groups with a presence in Libya—such as the various Ansar al-Sharia Libya branches and al Qa'ida in the Islamic Maghreb—also pose a threat to U.S. embassies and citizens in North Africa; so does al-Shabaab in Somalia. Its objectives are largely parochial: To establish an extreme Islamic emirate in Somalia and the broader region. Al-Shabaab possesses a competent external operations capability to strike targets in East Africa. The September 2013 Westgate Mall attack in Nairobi, Kenya, was well-planned and well-executed, and involved sophisticated intelligence collection, surveillance, and reconnaissance of the target.

Third, some extremist groups present a low-level threat to the United States. These groups do not possess the capability or intent to target the United States at home or overseas. They include such organizations as the East Turkestan Islamic Movement, which is primarily interested in Chinese targets.

III. FOREIGN FIGHTER CHALLENGE FROM SYRIA AND IRAQ

Of particular concern for the United States is the growing number of extremists—both Sunni and Shi'a—that have traveled to (and from) Syria and Iraq to fight. The Syrian-Iraqi battlefield likely has the largest concentration of foreign extremists of any jihadist battlefield in the modern era. There have been over 20,000 foreign fighters who have traveled to Syria to fight. Approximately 3,400 fighters, or 17 percent, appear to be coming from the West. Approximately 200 Americans are known to have attempted to travel to Syria to fight with Islamic militants.[8] It is difficult to predict whether most of the foreign fighters will remain in Syria, Iraq, and other countries over the long run to fight or die on the battlefield; move to future war zones; or return to the United States and other Western countries. Even if some return, it is uncertain whether they will become involved in terrorist plots, focus on recruiting and fundraising, or become disillusioned with terrorism. Still, foreign fighters have historically been agents of instability. Volunteering for war is often the principal stepping stone for individual involvement in more extreme forms of militancy—including in the United States.

Indeed, there have been a growing number of attacks and plots across the West tied either formally or informally to Syria and Iraq. These include attacks in Garland, Texas, in May 2015; Copenhagen, Denmark, in February 2015; Paris, France, in January 2015; Sydney, Australia, in December 2014; Ottawa, Canada, in October 2014; and Brussels, Belgium, in May 2014. More broadly, there were over 20 terrorist plots in the West either directed or provoked by extremist groups in Syria between October 2013 and January 2015.[9] Daesh has been linked directly or indirectly

---

[8] The data are from the National Counterterrorism Center. See Nicholas J. Rasmussen, *Current Terrorist Threat to the United States*: Hearing before the Senate Select Committee on Intelligence, February 12, 2015.

[9] The data are from the UK's Security Service, or MI5. See Andrew Parker, Director General of the Security Service (MI5), ''Terrorism, Technology and Accountability,'' Address to the Royal United Services Institute (RUSI) at Thames House, January 8, 2015.

to plots in such countries as France, Australia, Belgium, Libya, Tunisia, and the United States.[10]

There is also significant concern among America's European allies about the threat from Syria and Iraq. For instance, more than 600 British extremists have traveled to Syria and Iraq.[11] Many have joined Daesh. "We know that terrorists based in Syria harbor the same ambitions towards the United Kingdom—trying to direct attacks against our country, and exhorting extremists here to act independently," said MI5 director-general Andrew Parker in a January speech.[12] Similar to the United States, the British face a complex threat, with more extremists than MI5 and the Metropolitan Police Service's Counter Terrorism Command, or SO15, can cover at any one time. Despite these challenges, MI5 and the police remain aggressive. In England and Wales, there has been a 35-percent increase in terrorist-related arrests since 2011. And more than 140 individuals have been convicted for terrorism-related offenses since 2010.[13]

The British are not alone. Counterterrorism agencies across Europe and North America are under tremendous pressure to prevent terrorist attacks. French authorities report that nearly 1,400 French citizens have gone to Syria—or tried to go. French authorities arrested 91 persons suspected of extremist activity in 2012—and another 143 persons in 2013.[14]

IV. IMPLICATIONS FOR REFUGEES AND THE U.S. HOMELAND

Based on these threats, it is important to examine potential risks from increased refugee flows from the region. In February 2015, the Department of State noted that it was "likely to admit 1,000 to 2,000 Syrian refugees for permanent resettlement in Fiscal Year 2015 and a somewhat higher number, though still in the low thousands, in Fiscal Year 2016."[15]

Refugees have historically played—and will continue to play—a critical role in ensuring U.S. economic prosperity and cultural diversity. In addition, the threat to the U.S. homeland from refugees has been relatively low. Almost none of the major terrorist plots since 9/11 have involved refugees. Even in those cases where refugees were arrested on terrorism-related charges, years and even decades often transpired between their entry into the United States and their involvement in terrorism. In most instances, a would-be terrorist's refugee status had little or nothing to do with their radicalization and shift to terrorism.

But risks associated with refugees from Syria may be higher today for several reasons. First, Syria and neighboring Iraq have the highest numbers of foreign fighters on any modern jihadist battlefield, and there has already been an exodus of some fighters to the West. Second, several groups in the region like Daesh have planned to put operatives in the West, particularly in Europe, by having them seek political refugee status. Daesh has also been active in some refugee camps in Syria. Third, the U.S. intelligence community's understanding of extremists in Syria is worse than in many other jihadist battlefields, such as Iraq and Afghanistan, because of more limited intelligence collection capabilities.

Individual terrorists and terrorist groups have multiple options to attack the U.S. homeland. First, they can inspire and encourage locals to conduct attacks through magazines like *Dabiq* (published by Daesh) and *Inspire* (published by al Qa'ida in the Arabian Peninsula). Second, they can infiltrate members into the United States from overseas to conduct attacks or recruit operatives from U.S. communities. Third, they can target aircraft or vessels coming into the United States. In 2010, for example, al Qa'ida in the Arabian Peninsula attempted to target cargo planes using plastic explosives hidden in printer cartridges.

Refugees have occasionally been involved in the first two types of plots. Perhaps the best-known case involved Waad Ramadan and Alwan Mohanad Shareef Hammadi, who were arrested on Federal terrorism charges in 2009 in Bowling Green, Kentucky. They had been granted refugee status despite their insurgent activities in Iraq and their role in attacking U.S. troops. The Bowling Green arrests led to numerous changes in how the United States processed refugees and asylum-

---

[10] These attacks have generally not involved returned foreign fighters, but rather individuals inspired directly or indirectly by Daesh.

[11] Parker, 2015.

[12] Parker, 2015.

[13] Parker, 2015.

[14] Brian Michael Jenkins and Jean-Francois Clair, "Predicting the 'Dangerousness' of Potential Terrorists," *The Hill*, March 26, 2015; Jenkins and Clair, "Different Countries, Different Ways of Countering Terrorism," *The Hill*, February 27, 2015.

[15] Jen Psaki, U.S. State Department Daily Press Briefing, Washington, DC, February 13, 2015.

seekers. The process had been haphazard, partly because there were so many refugees and asylum-seekers—including from Iraq—being processed through the system. But there were also challenges because the data were not well organized across the U.S. Government.

Overall, there are a small number of cases in which refugees have been arrested on terrorism-related charges in the United States. Examples include the following:

- a Bosnian refugee in St. Louis (arrested in 2015)
- a Somali refugee in Minneapolis (2015)
- an Uzbek refugee in Boise, Idaho (2013)
- two Chechen refugees in Boston (2013)
- an Uzbek refugee in Aurora, Colorado (2012)
- two Iraqi refugees in Bowling Green, Kentucky (2011)
- a Somali refugee in Columbus, Ohio (2011)
- a Somali refugee in St. Louis, Missouri (2010)
- a Somali refugee in Portland, Oregon (2010)
- an Afghan refugee in Aurora, Colorado (2009)

There have been other cases in Canada. Ahmed Ressam, the millennium bomber who was convicted in 2001 of planning to bomb Los Angeles International Airport (LAX) on New Year's Eve 1999, had applied to Canada as a refugee. He was denied refugee status, but still managed to remain in Canada before attempting to attack the United States. Raed Jaser, who pled guilty in March 2015 to involvement in a terrorist plot that targeted a train route between Toronto and New York City, had applied for refugee status in Canada as a Palestinian. The Canadian government rejected his family's refugee claims. But since the family was stateless, the government allowed family members to stay in the country under Canada's "deferred removal" program. Finally, Sayfildin Tahir Sharif (also known as Faruq Khalil Muhammad 'Isa), who was arrested in Canada in 2011 on a U.S. warrant, had moved to Canada as a refugee from Iraq.

Because of these concerns, the United States should reassess its refugee program and make sure it safeguards National security. As already noted, a number of changes were implemented after the Bowling Green arrests. It is worth examining whether there needs to be enhanced screening and data collection for applicants, such as

- additional background checks and other screening protocols in place at the Department of Homeland Security and the Federal Bureau of Investigation for screening refugee applicants—including Syrian applicants—through the U.S. Refugee Admissions Program (USRAP).
- improved data management of potentially concerning refugees. Some of the mistakes in the past were not due to screening errors, but rather caused by poor data management. Information on terrorist links never made it to the right databases.
- an enhanced U.S. intelligence community role in implementing heightened measures to vet potential refugees from countries of concern, including Syria. Some of this has already occurred through such programs as the National Counterterrorism Center's Kingfisher Expansion program.
- enhanced re-screening procedures for refugees who have entered the United States
- better engagement with Visa Waiver Program countries out of concern that refugees from Syria, Iraq, or other high-risk countries could be resettled there and then enter the United States with a lower level of scrutiny
- additional authorities to hold data collected in refugee camps.

The United States has a long-standing tradition of offering protection and freedom to refugees who live in fear of persecution, some of whom are left to languish in deplorable conditions of temporary asylum. An integral part of that mission needs to be ensuring that those refugees considered for entry into the United States, including from such jihadist battlefields as Syria, do not present a risk to the safety and security of the United States.

Mr. KING. Thank you, Dr. Jones.

Our next witness, Tom Fuentes, served in the Federal Bureau of Investigation for 25 years, retiring in 2008 as an assistant director. His distinguished career focused particularly on organized crime, cyber crime, and international law enforcement cooperation. For any of us who watch television, he is currently serving as a law enforcement analyst for CNN. I am glad you took a break from the jailbreak itself today to join with us. Seriously, I certainly always get a lot out of listening to your commentaries and your analysis on these issues. It is a privilege to have you testifying here today. I thank you. Mr. Fuentes, you are recognized.

STATEMENT OF THOMAS FUENTES, ASSISTANT DIRECTOR (RETIRED), FEDERAL BUREAU OF INVESTIGATION

Mr. FUENTES. Thank you, Chairman King. Thank you, other Members of the committee, for inviting me here today. I did not submit a prepared statement in advance. I knew that my distinguished colleagues would very well illustrate the number of Syrian refugees, the scope of the issue of trying to determine how many will come, how they will come in, what processes will occur for them to try to vet them.

My point with this would be that the last 5 years of my career in the FBI, I served as the head of the International Program, running the legal attaché offices around the world. I was the Bureau's first on-scene commander in Iraq in 2003. I also served as a member of Interpol's executive committee and have worked closely with Interpol issues for more than 25 years.

The issue of international police cooperation is essential in everything we do. In all aspects of American business, students overseas, vacationers overseas, the issue of having countries that we work closely with, that we can rely on is essential for all aspects. But this particular issue, it comes down to do we have working partners in Syria. The fact is we do not.

When I was in charge in Iraq in the summer of 2003 into the fall of 2003, even simple things there became difficult because the looters had taken the computers of Iraq's Department of Motor Vehicles and other Government computers, the actual computers that had the data on them, and the servers. So we had no way to vet immediately in the summer of 2003, but we built that up over time as we had the intelligence assets. I opened the FBI's formal legal attaché office in October 2004. The United States has been able to work with Iraqis and get information.

We have had some success, again, in Afghanistan and other countries that we were working with. But currently in Syria, we don't have that capability. We do not have an FBI office. Our human sources are minimal. Our, obviously, signals intelligence are also going to be minimal to understand what is actually occurring there. We don't have a Government we can partner with. That is the key thing. If any of these individuals would be in a database, you know, that is why they are refugees in many cases. If they are on the Government's radar in Syria, it could be for negative reasons which would cause them to want to come out and possibly seek a life here.

So, for me, I would completely agree that the ideals of this country are that we take in immigrants and refugees from all over the world seeking the American Dream, seeking a better life, and especially the refugees that seek it for their children obviously. That becomes a problem as well when the children come, as we saw with the Somali refugees. As we saw in the Tsarnaev case, the Boston bombers, you see children who 4 or 5 years later are old enough to become radicalized even with their parents being completely unaware.

So my issue with this is how the vetting process would work, how it could possibly succeed, and recognizing that I know the FBI does not have the ability to really do an adequate vetting on this issue. Thank you.

Mr. KING. Thank you, Mr. Fuentes.

Our next witness, is Dr. Daveed Gartenstein-Ross, a senior fellow at the Foundation for Defense of Democracies, an adjunct professor at Georgetown University's Security Studies Program, and a lecturer at the Catholic University of America.

He is also the chief executive officer of Valens Global, a consulting firm focusing on the challenges posed by violent, non-state actors. Doctor, it is a privilege to have you here today. You are recognized. Thank you

STATEMENT OF DAVEED GARTENSTEIN-ROSS, SENIOR FELLOW, FOUNDATION FOR DEFENSE OF DEMOCRACIES

Mr. GARTENSTEIN-ROSS. Thank you, Chairman King, Ranking Member Vela, distinguished Members of the committee. In this testimony, I want to talk about how we have significant interests in alleviating the refugee situation in the region.

The refugee situation caused by the Syria conflict is very grave. Both for humanitarian reasons and also for reasons of National interest, we should care about the situation deeply. This committee has also quite clearly raised issues about domestic radicalization. I think declining domestic capacity is something that should be considered, as well as the overall coherence of our migration policies.

With respect to the region, as Dr. Jones said, there are about 4 million registered refugees outside of Syria right now. You also have a significant amount of, millions of Syrians who can be classified as internally displaced persons. You have significant upheaval and strain that this is causing in neighboring states. In Jordan, which is already a state which is strapped for water, which has a sky-high unemployment rate, in Lebanon, in Turkey, this has caused multiple challenges, both internal security challenges, domestic unrest, pitting native citizens against refugees. You have 155,000 registered refugees from Syria in North Africa and a significant movement of refugees into Europe from Libya's human trafficking networks. The collapse of the state in Libya has caused massive inflows through what is called the central Mediterranean route.

Now, when this committee looks at this situation, there is both, as I said, humanitarian concerns and also strategic concerns related to the impact this has on the United States' partners in the region. When we look at, however, the risks associated with this, I think there is two specific radicalization concerns. One which was already raised is the concern that you might try to insert, a terrorist group might try to insert operatives into the United States in this way. This is not, I would say, the primary concern in my view. The reason why is because in order to get an operative into the United States, a group like Jabhat al-Nusra or the Islamic State would have to land them in a refugee camp and then hope they got picked up in the lottery process, in this case, being considered one of the neediest by the United Nations and then move to the United States.

Now, this could happen. But there is much easier ways to move into Europe such as coming in through Libya, given the fact that a large number of Syrian refugees or those who can be classified as refugees are now moving into Europe through the Libyan route. However, despite the fact that I think the danger isn't particularly high, when you look at the security procedures, they are layered but they really look like the TSA's layered procedures, where the TSA checks a lot of boxes. But at the end of the day and the tests that have been done recently, it hasn't found the bomb. Other than the interview procedure, if that is done effectively, I am not convinced there is anything that really stands a chance of preventing a terrorist operative from getting in.

Now, the second thing is radicalization concerns. If you look at the narrative that could be used for a Syrian refugee, it is going to depend upon whether they were displaced by the Islamic State, by al-Nusra, or by the Assad regime which is extraordinarily brutal. I think we would be foolish to ignore the fact that not the Islamic State, but Jabhat al-Nusra, al-Qaeda's affiliate in Syria, has recently managed to position itself as at the forefront of opposing Assad and has managed to make itself popular both with other opposition groups and also with many Syrian people. For someone in the United States who has a special interest in Syria, sees the West as not acting, and looks at Nusra as cooperating with people, providing governance, and being at the forefront of opposing Assad, I think there is an elevated risk of radicalization that needs to be a part of this conversation.

The final two things I want to point to, our declining domestic capacity. When we talk about violent non-state actors in the United States of all stripes, one thing that is of concern is that our resources are going to become fewer and fewer in the future. We have a National debt that is skyrocketing, that should soon surpass $20 trillion. Right now, it is at the $18 trillion mark. Looking at our own resources to handle problems that exist within the United States should be part of any conversation that involves outlays both on the security and humanitarian end.

Finally, I want to say a word about the coherence of U.S. migration policies. I would say the United States has not met its basic obligations to people who helped us in Iraq and in Afghanistan, serving as translators or contractors for U.S. efforts. When we talk about taking in people from abroad, those who are needy, those who help the United States should be part of any conversation and should be at the forefront of those who we try to help. The United States deservedly has a bad reputation for not standing behind people who help us. When we deal with a situation where there are more conflicts at the sub-state level where we have to liaise with sub-state actors, making sure that we garner the right reputation for standing by our friends is an important part of what U.S. policy should promote.

[The prepared statement of Mr. Gartenstein-Ross follows:]

PREPARED STATEMENT OF DAVEED GARTENSTEIN-ROSS

JUNE 24, 2015

Chairman King, Ranking Member Higgins, and distinguished Members of the committee, on behalf of the Foundation for Defense of Democracies, it is an honor to appear before you to discuss the humanitarian and security issues posed by admitting Syrian refugees, and what the Government can do to address this challenge. The Syrian refugee crisis represents the tragic consequences of politics gone awry in the Middle East. Millions of Syrians have been displaced due to the fighting, which has also produced a near-complete fracturing of Syrian society. The refugee crisis must be considered with an emphasis on both humanitarian and security issues, as they are deeply linked. This testimony thus seeks to highlight the competing considerations that should inform our thinking and policies on this issue by focusing on both the deep humanitarian and geopolitical challenges associated with the Syrian refugee crisis, but also reasons why policymakers have legitimate concerns about the admission of large numbers of Syrian refugees into the United States. Even though rebel groups seem to have recently broken the stalemate with Bashar al-Assad's regime, this doesn't mean that the Syrian civil war will imminently end, and even an end of the civil war doesn't mean an end to the refugee crisis: The proliferation of jihadist groups in the country is a demonstration of just how enduring the refugee crisis may be.

The United States is now asking whether it should accept those Syrian refugees left most vulnerable by the conflict While there may be both moral and pragmatic considerations counseling in favor of such a course of action, there are also challenges involved in doing so, and the risk exists that the United States could end up with an incoherent set of migrations policies, given its failure to admit the many Afghans and Iraqis who directly aided U.S. efforts during the major wars in both countries. *Put simply, the United States has not met its obligation to locals in those two countries who assisted the U.S. military efforts, and whose lives are endangered as a result. Thus, any discussion of admitting Syrian refugees should recognize these obligations as a part of the discussion, one that should take priority.*

My testimony begins by outlining, country by country, the impacts of the Syrian refugee crisis, detailing where refugees have ended up in the Middle East, Europe, and North America. It examines the conditions of refugee camps, as well as humanitarian efforts of host nations and international organizations. The Jordanian response will be specifically highlighted, as Jordan has been particularly challenged by the sudden influx of refugees. The testimony concludes by describing potential problems related to resettling Syrian refugees in the United States, including security concerns.

THE HUMANITARIAN CRISIS RELATED TO SYRIAN REFUGEES

The Syrian refugee crisis, now entering its fourth year, presents dire humanitarian concerns. The exodus of Syrians to neighboring states has created a myriad of challenges for host countries and aid organizations alike. Syrians displaced from the conflict now number almost 4 million in such neighboring countries such as Turkey, Lebanon, Jordan, Iraq, and Egypt, as well as European and North American states.

Syrian refugees have been removed from the violence that continues to plague their home country, but they remain an at-risk population in the countries to which they have fled. Conditions in refugee camps vary, but they have created numerous humanitarian issues. Outside of the camps, displaced Syrians struggle to afford housing and find work, while host nations grapple with the implications of trying to integrate a refugee population that has become more likely to stay as the crisis continues.

Scope of the crisis.—According to the U.N. High Commissioner for Refugees (UNHCR), the UN's refugee agency, nearly 4 million registered Syrian refugees live outside of Syria.[1] There is also an unknown, though sizable, number of Syrian refugees who have not been registered, leaving them in legal limbo and without access to services provided by humanitarian agencies. Additionally, the Internal Displacement Monitoring Centre (IDMC) estimates that there are approximately 7.6 million

---

[1] The UN High Commissioner for Refugees, ''Syria Regional Refugee Response,'' May 31, 2015, available at *http://data.unhcr.org/syrian-efugees/regional.php.*

internally displaced persons (IDPs) in Syria, making it the country with the largest population of individuals displaced by conflict and violence in the world.[2]

Countries bordering Syria have borne most of the burden of housing Syrian refugees. Turkey, with over 1.7 million registered refugees, holds more registered Syrian refugees than any other country. Second to Turkey is Lebanon, which houses nearly 1.2 million registered refugees, along with approximately 300,000 unregistered refugees.[3] Jordan houses approximately 620,000 refugees, with the majority (80 percent) residing in urban areas such as the capital, Amman.[4] Iraq houses around 250,000 Syrian refugees, in addition to 3 million-plus IDPs who have been displaced by the current conflict in Iraq.[5]

Syrian refugees have also sought asylum or temporary residency in other countries in the region. According to UNHCR, there are 155,000 registered Syrian refugees in North Africa; of those, approximately 130,000 reside in Egypt, though conditions for Syrian refugees in that country have deteriorated since Mohamed Morsi's regime was overthrown in July 2013.[6] A growing number of Syrian refugees based in Egypt have attempted the treacherous journey to Europe by sea. A significant number of Syrian refugees also live in Libya, though most of them are unregistered. Many Syrian refugees still residing in Libya do not intend to remain, and are planning to travel to Europe via Libya's well-established human smuggling networks.[7]

Europe is home to a steadily-growing population of Syrian refugees. Nearly 150,000 Syrians have sought asylum in Europe since 2011 and European Union (E.U.) member states have pledged to resettle another 33,000 Syrians in the coming months.[8] Though E.U. law states that refugees must register in their country of entry, many Syrian refugees evade migration officials in southern and eastern European countries, and travel to northern European countries, where they then apply for asylum. Among European states, Germany and Sweden have received the most Syrian refugees, with both countries processing over 50,000 Syrian asylum applications from 2011–2014.[9] Of the 33,000 refugees whom E.U. member states have vowed to resettle, the vast majority (30,000) will be resettled in Germany.[10]

The United States has admitted a small number of Syrian refugees. According to the State Department, 700 Syrian refugees have been accepted since the civil war began, and the State Department has revealed plans to accept as many as 2,000 additional refugees by the fall of 2015.[11] Canada has pledged to accept 11,000 refugees in the near future.

Conditions for refugees inside and outside of refugee camps.—The massive forced migration out of Syria has necessitated a huge humanitarian response. Camps have been established in several countries to address the inflow of refugees. Yet with dwindling funds and resources, conditions are deteriorating.

There are over 3.5 million Syrian refugees in Jordan, Iraq, Turkey, and Lebanon. Camps provide food, water, electricity, cash vouchers, basic medical services, education, and shelter. The camps, and the services they provide, are jointly managed by the host governments, UNHCR, and several participating NGOs. Some camps,

---

[2] Internal Displacement Monitoring Centre, "Syria IDP Figures Analysis," December 2014, available at *http://www.internal-displacement.org/middle-east-and-north-africa/syria/; Global Overview 2014: People Internally Displaced by Conflict and Violence* (Geneva: Norwegian Refugee Council and Internal Displacement Monitoring Centre, May 2014), p. 11, available at *http://www.internal-displacement.org/assets/publications/2014/201405-global-overview-2014-en.pdf.* Note: The distinction between IDPs and refugees is that refugees have fled their country of citizenship, whereas IDPs have left their home but remain in their country of citizenship.

[3] Nour Samaha, " 'I Wasn't Afraid, but Now I Am': Syrians Fear Lebanon's Visa Rules," *Al Jazeera,* January 5, 2015.

[4] European University Institute and Migration Policy Centre, "Syrian Refugees: A Snapshot of the Crisis—in the Middle East and Europe," August 2014, available at *http://syrianrefugees.eu/?pagelid=87.*

[5] Internal Displacement Monitoring Centre, "Iraq IDP Figures Analysis," January 2015, available at *http://www.internal-displacement.org/middle-east-and-north-africa/iraq/.*

[6] Tom Rollins, "Syrian Refugees in Egypt Determined to Get to Europe," *Al-Monitor,* July 24, 2014.

[7] "What's Behind the Surge in Refugees Crossing the Mediterranean Sea," *New York Times,* May 21, 2015.

[8] European University Institute and Migration Policy Centre, "Syrian Refugees: A Snapshot of the Crisis."

[9] Harriet Grant, "UN Plan to Relocate Syrian Refugees in Northern Europe," *Guardian* (U.K.), March 11, 2015.

[10] United Nations High Commissioner for Refugees, "Resettlement and Other Forms of Admission for Syrian Refugees." May 13, 2015, available at *http://www.unhcr.org/52b2febafc5.pdf.*

[11] Somini Sengupta, "U.N. Calls on Western Nations to Shelter Syrian Refugees," *New York Times,* April 17, 2015.

notably the Kilis camp in Turkey have relatively high standards of living.[12] But the quality of services is not standardized across all camps; and even in a well-run camp like Kilis, the refugees want nothing more than to leave.[13] Many camps have seen overcrowding and major budget shortfalls, and some camps reportedly lack electricity.[14] Malnutrition, poverty, and disease are endemic.

But these camps represent the living situation for only 11 percent of refugees. Eighty-nine percent live in communities outside the camps, among the native population. Egypt and Lebanon, both of which have accepted a large number of refugees, do not even have official camps. The sudden influx of refugees has caused tensions with local populations, in part due to rising property costs, unemployment rates, and the overburdening of public institutions such as health care and education. Indeed, conditions outside of the camps are arguably worse for Syrian refugees than conditions within the camps. A recent report by UNHCR concerning the refugees in Jordan living outside of official camps (84% of the total for that country) found that nearly half were living in bad or uninhabitable conditions, two-thirds were living at or below the poverty line, and one-sixth lived in abject poverty.[15] Refugees living outside of official camps lack many of the essential services that are at least partially provided inside the camps. This has caused even further substandard living conditions for Syrian refugees who resettle among the native population.

Conditions for refugees, both inside and outside of official camps, are likely to worsen. Only 20 percent of the $4.5 billion funding request for UNHCR to sustain its 2015 operations assisting refugees has been fulfilled.[16] Food aid has already been cut, as the Associated Press explains:

"The World Food Program reduced the number of Syrian refugees eligible for food vouchers from 1.9 million to 1.7 million in January to focus on the neediest. Since then, it has twice reduced benefits, most recently in May by a total of about 30 percent, and the neediest among more than 520,000 refugees living outside camps in Jordan now receive just $21 per person per month."[17]

The situation can be expected to further deteriorate. Lacking money and resources, UNHCR and host governments will not be able to sustain their current efforts without more assistance from the international community.

The case of Jordan.—The impact of Jordanian refugees on Jordan demonstrates that the current crisis is not just humanitarian, but also has real strategic implications for the region—and for the United States as well. Jordan's current population is approximately 8 million, of which about 628,160 are Syrian refugees.[18] This 8.5 percent increase in population attributable to the inflow of refugees from Syria has strained the country in multiple ways.

Most Syrian refugees have settled in either Jordan's urban centers or refugee camps, with about 80% going to urban areas. A statistical analysis my research team performed on Syrian refugees in Jordan suggests that 51.3 percent are in the northern region, while only 3.5 percent are in the south; and the distribution of Syrian refugees in Jordan is even more uneven on a governorate scale. The Mafraq governorate, which makes up most of Jordan's border with Syria, has absorbed most of the refugees in the north, and 25% of all Syrian refugees in Jordan overall. Refugees now make up 35% of Mafraq's population, with the two major destinations being the capital city of Mafraq and the Za'atari refugee camp.

Syrian refugees in Jordanian cities, initially welcomed with a high degree of hospitality, are encountering rising tensions with the host community. A September 2012 report showed that 80% of Jordanians in the city of Mafraq would prefer that the refugees leave the city to live in camps.[19] The rising population produced by the

[12] Mac McClelland, "How to Build a Perfect Refugee Camp," *New York Times,* February 13, 2014.

[13] Ibid.

[14] Michael Kimmelman, "Refugee Camp for Syrians in Jordan Evolves as a Do-It-Yourself City," *New York Times,* July 4, 2014 (discussing the Azraq camp).

[15] United Nations High Commissioner for Refugees, *Living in the Shadows: Jordan Home Visits Report 2014* (January 2015), available at *http://www.unhcr.org/54b685079.pdf.*

[16] Data taken from the United Nations High Commissioner for Refugees, "Syria Regional Refugee Response," last updated May 31, 2015, at *http://data.unhcr.org/syrianrefugees/regional.php.*

[17] "Syrian Refugees Struggle Amid Aid Cuts, Lack Labor Rights," Associated Press, May 19, 2015.

[18] UNHCR, "Syria Regional Refugee Response: Jordan," May 28, 2015, at *http://data.unhcr.org/syrianrefugees/country.php?id=107.*

[19] Elena Buryan, *Analysis of Host Community-Refugee Tensions in Mafraq, Jordan,* MercyCorps, October 2012.

inflow of refugees has caused, among other things, a drastic rise in housing prices.[20] Many Jordanians also fear that Syrian refugees are competing for their jobs.

Conditions in Jordanian refugee camps, especially the Za'atari camp—with 85,000 residents—are comparatively well-suited for a long-term stay, and the camps have appeared more permanent over time. (This is not to say that the conditions can be considered good.) Za'atari has a significant black market economy, but also signs of normalcy that include barber shops, paved streets, electric poles, private toilets, private gardens, a pet store, a flower shop, and an ice cream parlor. In July 2014, 3,500 businesses could be found in Za'atari.[21] Another indicator of the camps' potential permanence is rising levels of school attendance. One resident observed that most parents kept their children out of school initially, electing to wait and continue their education once they returned to Syria. Now, however, Za'atari residents send their children to school "because they don't have any hope to go back."[22] Jordan's government has begun to acknowledge, at least implicitly, that Syrian refugees could be permanent in the country. UNHCR's external relations officer noted that the new Azraq refugee camp is designed to function like a city instead of a temporary camp.[23]

This refugee population has placed significant demands on Jordan's resources. The government of Jordan is currently able to satisfy the basic needs of the refugee community, but it may not be able to do so in the long run. Jordan is one of the most water-scarce countries in the world, and before refugees arrived the country's groundwater resources were on track to be depleted as early as 2060.[24] The government's strategy to manage water use and increase sustainability did not account for the sudden addition of large numbers of Syrian refugees to the population. Water resources could now depleted years earlier than previously projected.

The locations hardest hit by the refugee influx have seen average daily supply of water per person plummet to 30 liters, far below the 80 liters per day necessary to satisfy basic needs. At this level, "sanitation standards decline, diseases rise, subsistence crops wither, and children go thirsty."[25] In Za'atari, refugees are allocated 35 liters of water per day, compared to the 70 to 145 liters per person per day provided in pre-conflict Syria.[26]

The entry of hundreds of thousands of Syrian refugees has caused food prices to rise sharply, especially in the north. For example, in Mafraq governorate, food prices have increased by 27 percent.[27] A study has found that more than 60 percent of Syrian refugees in the al-Ramtha, Beni Obaid, Irbid, and al-Badiya districts and the Jarash and Ajloun governorates do not have adequate access to food.[28] Compounding this problem has been substantial cuts in food assistance to Syrian refugees, as the World Food Program reduced the number of Syrian refugees eligible for food aid in January 2015, and has further reduced benefits twice since then.[29]

Further, the electricity generation sector has been strained, which has been expensive for Jordan's government due to its subsidization of energy.[30] Compounding the problem, Jordan imports 96 percent of its oil and gas, so it is exposed to fluctuations in energy prices on the supply side, and to population changes and increased consumption on the demand side.[31] Pressure on Jordan's sanitation, education, and health systems is also increasing.[32] Many schools are running two shifts at the expense of quality to accommodate Syrian refugee children, who are perceived to be

---

[20] Ibid.

[21] Kimmelman, "Refugee Camp for Syrians in Jordan Evolves as a Do-It-Yourself City."

[22] Alice Speri, " 'We Don't Have Any Hope to Go Back': Syrian Refugees' Lives Turn Permanent in Zaatari Camp," *Vice*, May 9, 2014.

[23] Ibid.

[24] "Tapped Out: Water Scarcity and Refugee Pressures in Jordan," Mercy Corps, March 2014.

[25] Ibid.

[26] Alaa Milbes, "Getting Water to Zaatari During Drought Season," Oxfam Policy and Practice Blog, August 19, 2014, at *www.policy-practice.oxfam.org.uk/blog/2014/08/getting-water-to-zaatari-during-drought-season.*

[27] Food and Agricultural Organisation, "Plan of Action: Jordan, 2014–2018," January 2014, at *www.fao.org/fileadmin/user/upload/rne/docs/Jordan-Plan.pdf.*

[28] Ibid.

[29] Karin Laub, "Syrian Refugees Struggle Amid Aid Cuts, Lack of Labor Rights," Associated Press, May 19, 2015.

[30] Khalid Al Wazani, *The Socio-Economic Implications of Syrian Refugees on Jordan: A Cost-Benefit Framework* (Amman: Issnaad Consulting, 2014), available at *www.kas.de/wf/doc/kas\37808-1522-2-30.pdf?140522145513.*

[31] U.S. Commercial Service, U.S. Department of Commerce, "Jordan: Renewable Energy Market," 2011, available at *http://export.gov/jordan/static/Jordan%20Renewable%-20Energy%20Market\Latest\eg\jol034925.doc.*

[32] Wazani, *The Socio-Economic Implications of Syrian Refugees on Jordan.*

at a lower educational level than Jordanian children due to curriculum differences and their interruption in education.

The influx of refugees also places significant strains on Jordan's economy. A January 2014 USAID study estimated that the direct and indirect costs of managing the Syrian refugee population amounted to 2.4 percent of Jordan's GDP.[33] The study found that growing government expenditures on refugees caused a decline in Jordan's ability to provide services and security to the general population.[34] A separate study by the U.N. Development Programme found that the cost of hosting refugees in Jordan totaled $5.3 billion for 2013–2014, and most of these costs were covered by Jordan's government.[35] And refugee-related economic costs extend to several other sectors of Jordan's economy. As previously noted, rental prices have increased as Syrian refugees drive up demand for rental units.[36] The uptick in rental prices, along with other factors related to the refugee population, has contributed to a rise in inflation. Jordan's informal economy has also expanded as Syrian refugees look for jobs in informal industries.

All of this has fueled resentment among native Jordanians, who have consistently opposed opening their border to Syrian refugees. In a survey conducted in 2013, 71 percent of Jordanians opposed allowing more Syrian refugees into the country, while 58 percent said that the quality of service had declined in neighborhoods where Syrian refugees lived.[37] Resentment and opposition to the refugee presence has only grown over time.

Jordan has been forced to adapt its policies to deal with the growing number of Syrian refugees residing within its borders. Jordan initially welcomed Syrian refugees with what can be termed an "open-border policy" at the start of the conflict in 2011. But as the Syria crisis intensified and became more protracted, Jordan has adjusted its control over the Jordan-Syria border, its management of refugee camps, and its legal framework concerning Syrian refugees. In September and October of 2014, for example, the border was closed to refugees, though the government's official stance remained that it was open to women, children, and injured refugees.[38] In November, Human Rights Watch found that Syrian refugees attempting to cross into Jordan were being forcibly returned.[39] Jordan again closed its border with Syria at the beginning of April 2015 due to the nearby outbreak of violence.[40] Jordan also began restricting the movement of Syrian refugees to urban areas by impeding their ability to exit camps and move around the country in 2014.

For these reasons, the Syrian refugee crisis is not just a humanitarian concern, but a strategic concern for one of the key U.S. allies in the region.

CONCERNS RELATED TO ACCEPTING MORE SYRIAN REFUGEES INTO THE UNITED STATES

The biggest concern related to the United States admitting greater numbers of Syrian refugees is that it has failed to meet its basic obligations to foreign nationals who assisted U.S. efforts in Iraq and Afghanistan. Only a fraction of the Afghans who served U.S. military efforts, including as interpreters or contractors, have been admitted into the United States.[41] Emerson Brooking and Janine Davidson note that "when American servicemen rotate away," their "translators remain—often becoming top-priority targets for reprisal attacks."[42]

The United States has a fundamental obligation to the men and women who worked with us in Iraq and Afghanistan, risking their lives and their families' lives.

---

[33] USAID, *The Fiscal Impact of the Syrian Refugee Crisis on Jordan* (January 2014), p. xi.

[34] Ibid., p. 38.

[35] United Nations Development Programme, *Municipal Needs Assessment Report: Mitigating the Impact of the Syrian Refugee Crisis on Jordanian Vulnerable Host Communities* (2014), p. 11.

[36] Yasser Abdih, Andrea Gamba, and Rafik Selma, *Jordan: Selected Issues* (Washington, DC: International Monetary Fund, April 2014), p. 5.

[37] Khaled Neimat, "Majority of Jordanians Call for End to Syrian Refugee Influx," *Jordan Times*, April 15, 2013.

[38] Rana Sweis, "No Syrians Are Allowed Into Jordan, Agencies Say," *New York Times*, October 8, 2014.

[39] Human Rights Watch, "Jordan: Vulnerable Refugees Forcibly Returned to Syria," November 24, 2014, at *http://www.hrw.org/news/2014/11/23/jordan-vulnerable-refugees-forcibly-returned-syria*.

[40] Suleiman al-Khalidi, "Jordan Shuts Border Crossing with Syria after Fighting," Reuters, April 1, 2015.

[41] Peter Cobus, "Where the Grave Isn't Free: One Afghan Interpreter's Trials of U.S. Resettlement," Voice of America, Apr 22, 2015.

[42] Emerson Brooking and Janine Davidson, "Why is a Comedian the Only One Talking About the Plight of Afghan Interpreters?," Council on Foreign Relations, October 23, 2014, available at *http://blogs.cfr.org/davidson/2014/10/23/why-is-a-comedian-the-only-one-talking-about-the-plight-of-afghan-interpreters/*.

The situation for refugees from Syria is tragic, and is important for many reasons. But as we focus on the current crisis, let us not forget those to whom we owe a direct debt: There are both moral and also pragmatic reasons that we should put them at the top of our migration priorities. Further, one concern policymakers have about admitting Syrian refugees is whether some militants might be in their midst, and the Afghans and Iraqis who helped the United States should present a lower vetting burden.[43]

Beyond the concern that the United States should ensure that Afghans and Iraqis who assisted U.S. efforts should not be left home to die, there are pragmatic concerns related to increasing our admission of Syrian refugees. The first one this testimony will discuss is terrorism and lawlessness concerns.

Policies for screening refugees.—The United States has a set of layered policies in place for screening and admitting refugees. The system involves multiple checks across several agencies for medical and security concerns. Though this lessens the probability that malevolent actors will gain entrance into the United States, it fundamentally depends on the quality of U.S. intelligence about the Syrian refugee population. The biggest concern is a "clean skin," an individual connected with a jihadist organization whose connections to the group are not known by American intelligence or law enforcement agencies. Indeed, U.S. officials have expressed concern that they might lack the assets to properly vet Syrian refugees for ties with militant groups prior to resettlement in the United States. As FBI assistant director Michael Steinbach said, "You have to have information to vet. Databases don't [have] the information on those individuals, and that's the concern."[44]

The White House has allotted up to 70,000 refugees for permanent resettlement in fiscal year 2015, with 33,000 places reserved for refugees from the Middle East and South Asia.[45] Syrian refugees are now seen as of special humanitarian concern to the United States, as both UNHCR and the United States have determined that "tens of thousands of refugees living outside Syria are unlikely to ever be able to return."[46] The UN's high commissioner on refugees, Antonio Guterres, has called on industrialized countries to admit 130,000 Syrian refugees in the next 2 years.[47] Candidates for resettlement to the United States have been referred by UNHCR, and there are currently 11,000 refugees who will be screened by U.S. officials as the next step in the process.[48] The UN's refugee agency has said that those on the United States' list include "the most vulnerable," such as single mothers and their children, victims of torture, and people with medical needs; and they also include Syrians who have worked with Americans, thus making them vulnerable to persecution.[49]

To be admissible, a candidate must pass a series of security and medical checks. A Department of State Resettlement Service Center (RSC) compiles personal data and background information for the security check process [50] Some refugees go through an additional review, a Security Advisory Opinion, which is conducted by multiple law enforcement and intelligence agencies. While the methodology for additional review selection is not public, it is reasonable to assume that those who are flagged as potentially posing a more severe security threat are selected. Candidates for refugee status are also fingerprinted and interviewed in person by an officer from U.S. Citizenship and Immigration Services. A medical screening is completed, mostly to check for infectious diseases such as tuberculosis. Finally, a second interagency security check is completed before the refugee's departure to verify that all information remains correct, and that there are no relevant additions since the process began. Only after all these security and medical checks have been completed and analyzed can a refugee be admitted to the United States.

[43] Rusty Bradley, "Heroes Left to Die," *War on the Rocks,* April 23, 2014.

[44] Justin Fishel and Mike Levine, "U.S. Officials Admit Concern over Syrian Refugee Effort," ABC News, February 12, 2015.

[45] Lauren Gambino, "U.S. Steps up Syrian Refugee Admissions, But Why Are Some Still Excluded?," *Guardian* (U.K.), March 11, 2015.

[46] Anne Gearan, "U.S. to Greatly Expand Resettlement for Syrian Refugees," *Washington Post,* September 30, 2014.

[47] Somini Sengupta, "U.N. Calls on Western Nations to Shelter Syrian Refugees," *New York Times,* April 17, 2015.

[48] Ibid.

[49] See ibid. (discussing how those on the list are among the most vulnerable); Gearan, "U.S. to Greatly Expand Resettlement" (discussing the inclusion of Syrians who have worked with Americans).

[50] The various steps of the refugee settlement process are outlined in U.S. Committee for Refugees and Immigrants, "Security Screening of Refugees Admitted to the United States: A Detailed, Rigorous Process," n.d., available at *www.rcusa.org/uploads/pdfs/Refugee%20resettlement%20-%20step%20by%20step%20USCRI.pdf.*

The process of resettling to the United States as a refugee can take as few as 8 weeks, but on average it takes 18 to 24 months.[51] However, the Department of State can expedite the process if there is a need, including particular physical dangers to the refugees.

After refugees are approved for resettlement, they receive U.S. Government support for moving and transitioning to life in the United States. Though refugees are not given the option to pick where they will live initially, if they have relatives in the United States, they will likely be resettled with or near them.[52] Otherwise, domestic resettlement agencies match the resource capabilities of around 190 available communities to refugee needs in order to find the best match. Various State and Federal agencies, in conjunction with private organizations, are responsible for supporting refugees through the resettlement process. Refugees are met at the airport, taken to their new apartment, and given appliances, climate-appropriate clothing, food, and a one-time sum to help with initial expenses.[53] Refugees can work immediately upon arrival in the United States. With proper documentation, trips outside the country permitted, but the refugees are not allowed to return to their country of persecution.[54] One year after resettlement, refugees are required to apply for permanent residency, and after 5 years in the United States they can apply for citizenship.

Security concerns.—There has been a great deal of concern related to the current influx of refugees into Europe, which is degrees of magnitude larger than the United States' intake of refugees. Counterterrorism officials and even some refugees have warned that militant groups such as the Islamic State may seek to infiltrate Western Europe. One refugee in Germany warned about Italy's lax security measures: "Any ISIS terrorist could have entered Italy and traveled further into Europe without any problem. ISIS members can take their guns and hand grenades with them, because the Italians never even checked any of the luggage."[55] Islamic State supporters have similarly alluded to their interest in using migrant outflows to gain entry into Europe.[56] Though security concerns are lower for the United States, they should still be acknowledged.

There are several cases of refugees who have been involved in terrorist activities in the United States, though the risks should not be exaggerated. In May 2011, Waad Alwan and Mohanad Hammadi, two Iraqi refugees who had been resettled in Kentucky, were arrested in a sting operation and charged with attempting to provide arms to al-Qaeda in Iraq (the group that would later become the Islamic State). In talks with an undercover informant, the men also discussed the possibility of carrying out attacks domestically. Both Alwan and Hammadi are believed to have been involved in the Sunni insurgency in Iraq before coming to the United States: Hammadi even boasted to an undercover operative involved in the sting operation that he had planted IEDs in Iraq, while Alwan told the same operative that he had killed U.S. soldiers with a sniper rifle.[57] Both men were admitted into the United States despite having been detained in Iraq due to suspicions about their involvement in insurgent activities.[58]

Tamerlan and Dzokhar Tsarnaev, the brothers responsible for the Boston Marathon bombing, arrived in the United States after their parents received refugee status in 2002.[59] Tamerlan was 15 and Dzokhar was 8 at the time. They would subsequently radicalize and carry out their notorious attack.

Though distinct from the above instances due to the differences between the admission of refugees and asylum seekers, several jihadists involved in terrorist activities in the United States used asylum applications to remain in the country. Mir Aimal Kansi, who shot and killed 2 CIA employees and wounded 3 more in a January 1993 attack outside the agency's Langley headquarters, entered the United

[51] U.S. Department of State, "U.S. Refugee Admissions Program," n.d., available at *http://www.state.gov/j/prm/ra/admissions/*.

[52] U.S. Department of State, "The Reception and Placement Program," n.d., available at *http://www.state.gov/j/prm/ra/reception-placement/index.htm*.

[53] Ibid.

[54] U.S. Citizenship and Immigration Services, Department of Homeland Security, "Refugees," April 11, 2013, available at *http://www.uscis.gov/humanitarian/refugees-asylum/refugees*.

[55] Harald Doornbos and Jenan Moussa, "Italy Opens the Door to Disaster," *Foreign Policy*, April 13, 2015.

[56] See discussion in Charlie Winter, *Libya: The Strategic Gateway for the Islamic State* (London: Quilliam Foundation, 2015).

[57] Carrie Johnson, "Terrorism Case Exposes Gaps In Refugee Screening," NPR, June 8, 2011.

[58] James Gordon Meek, Cindy Galli, and Brian Ross, "Exclusive: U.S. May Have Let 'Dozens' of Terrorists into Country As Refugees," ABC News, November 20, 2013.

[59] Peter Finn, Carol Leonnig, and Will Englund, "Tamerlan Tsarnaev and Dzhokhar Tsarnaev Were Refugees from Brutal Chechen Conflict," *Washington Post*, April 19, 2013.

States illegally but applied for asylum, and was later allowed to stay in the country under a general immigration amnesty. Omar Abdel Rahman applied for political asylum to delay his deportation.[60] Similarly, Ramzi Yousef, a key leader of the 1993 World Trade Center attack, ''asked for asylum and was released pending a hearing,'' and organized the attack while his asylum application was still pending.[61]

Post-traumatic stress and other vulnerabilities.—Syrian refugees have been particularly susceptible to post-traumatic stress disorder (PTSD) because of their exposure to warfare, detachment from their previous life, and the privations of refugee life. They have continued to face hardships even after escaping a war zone. According to recent academic study on Syrian refugees, up to a third of Syrian refugees suffer from PTSD.[62] PTSD can serve as a major impediment to successful integration into society, including manifesting in adjustment issues, language barriers, unemployment, and feelings of isolation and exclusion. PTSD sufferers often experience severe anxiety, panic attacks, insomnia, and erratic behavior. These symptoms can reveal themselves through difficulty in completing daily tasks, difficulty in school, substance abuse, and suicidal thoughts.[63] Beyond PTSD, refugees' experiences with losing their home, family, friends, and livelihood can produce their own sets of problems.

CONCLUSION

Thus, the Syrian refugee crisis presents a large number of challenges, both humanitarian and strategic. As I said at the outset, the United States should link its refugee policies to fulfilling our obligations to Iraqis and Afghans who assisted U.S. efforts in those countries. Fulfilling U.S. obligations to Iraqis and Afghans who assisted U.S. war efforts should be seen as of paramount importance for both moral and pragmatic reasons.

As this testimony has demonstrated, there are a variety of considerations related to Syrian refugees, and while security considerations should not be overstated, they do exist. (Some of the specifics of the refugee population being considered for refugee status, such as the fact that it represents the most vulnerable members, may mitigate concerns about terrorism and radicalization.) In addition to considering options related to refugee resettlement, U.S. policy makers should look to crafting comprehensive policies that also address such matters as targeted investments to alleviate the economic hardship on countries with large refugee populations, measures such as improved education to enhance the quality of life for Syrian refugees, and appropriate law enforcement training for countries hosting these populations.

Thank you again for inviting me to testify today. I look forward to answering your questions.

Mr. KING. Thank you, Doctor.

I would just add that to the extent that I am familiar with that issue, I fully agree with the last point you made, that we have not done enough for those who, especially in Afghanistan, the translators who are going to be left behind. They are at risk from the Taliban and others. I fully agree with that statement.

You mentioned the importance of countries in the region, that we assist them with the, in fact, you mentioned, let me also ask the question to all three members of the panel, I have Jordan in mind in particular, how important it is that we do something to alleviate the pressure in Jordan. At the same time, we have these real risks to the United States.

How much faith would any of the three of you have if we focused on the refugees in Jordan and relied for assistance on the Jordanian Government as far as vetting? It would seem to me we

[60] Ted Conover, ''The United States of Asylum,'' *New York Times*, September 19, 1993.

[61] Daryl Fears, ''Bill Shifts Burden to Asylum-Seekers,'' *Washington Post*, May 1, 2005. Both Kansi and Yousef exploited an asylum process that, at the time, allowed any migrant who applied for asylum to receive a work permit while his claim was being investigated. Following Kansi's attack, the United States eliminated asylum seekers' ability to do so.

[62] Gotay Alpak et al, ''Post-Traumatic Stress Disorder among Syrian Refugees in Turkey: A Cross-Sectional Study,'' *International Journal of Psychiatry in Clinical Practice* 19(1), March 2015, pp. 45–50.

[63] Claudia Maria Vargas, ''War Trauma in Refugees: Red Flags and Clinical Principles,'' *Visions: BC's Mental Health and Addictions Journal* 3(3), Winter 2007.

would have a better chance of vetting those refugees who have been in the camps in Jordan than we would just taking other refugees. I mean it is still a risk.

But do you believe it would serve a purpose to focus on refugees that are right now in Jordan and have gone through a certain vetting process from the Jordanians?

Mr. GARTENSTEIN-ROSS. The Jordanians, obviously, have a strong intelligence service. But the danger that we are talking about here is a refugee who could be classified as a clean skin. That is, if they don't have identifiable links to various terrorist organizations in the region. I think it is fair to assume, although I find that often when I assume things with the U.S. Government I really shouldn't, but it is fair to assume that there is already liaisons going on with Jordanian intelligence. So that if someone is flagged as being connected to Nusra or connected to ISIS, that we can get that information from the Jordanians.

So I think that to the extent that there is identifiable information, our layered screening procedure will pick that up. The problem is that we have a layered screening procedure which is not well-designed to pick up the clean skin. I think liaising with Jordanian intelligence doesn't solve that problem.

Mr. KING. Mr. Fuentes and Dr. Jones.

Mr. FUENTES. I think I would agree with that. We have had a very outstanding relationship with the Jordanians. I know I worked closely with them back during the time of the beginning of the Iraq war onward. Their intelligence service is excellent. They were inundated during the Iraq war time by hundreds of thousands of Iraqi refugees that poured into Jordan. Now they have equal numbers of Syrians, if not more, pouring in.

But the problem for the Jordanians is a similar problem for us, do they have access to intelligence on the ground to be able to vet people through Syria? Do they have enough of a relationship with Assad and is that enough for us to be able to rely on? I think one of the countries in the region that we have had a lot of success, surprisingly, has been Yemen. Even though we have removed many of the assets that we had in Yemen, we have been able to still rely on the outstanding work of the Saudi Arabians in Yemen. Because many of the Yemeni-Iraqi in the Arabian Peninsula members are Saudis. They were able to infiltrate that group from the beginning. They provide tremendous intelligence to the United States, to the British, to other services based on that.

A good example of that would be the printer cartridge bombs that were mailed to the United States, destined for the United States and for Western Europe. They had the exact shipping document numbers of each box. That enabled the British services at the airport there to actually open the box and find 80 grams of PETN. They have had success but that is because we have a service on the ground there that has already penetrated many of the groups in that country.

We don't have a similar situation in Syria. That is the big problem right now. We don't have any other reliable partner of ours that is already in that country in a position to supply us the information where if they were to get it, they would. But we don't know if they can get it.

Mr. KING. Dr. Jones.

Mr. JONES. Mr. Chairman, I think when you look at the refugee flows from Syria into the region, the highest numbers are in Turkey at about 1.7 million, in Lebanon, about 1.2 million, in Jordan, about 629,000, and then in Iraq, about 249,000 Syrian refugees. Out of those four countries, I would have notable concerns about the, what you are talking about in Turkey, Jordan, and Lebanon which brings me to Jordan.

The way I would answer your question is among those four major countries, Jordan has, I think, by far the best intelligence agency and the best handle on this problem for a range of reasons, including concerns about the destabilization of Jordan. So I would look at this as almost a layered defense. We took a chunk of the refugees from Jordan, I think they have got better access to intelligence on refugees. We would also rely on U.S. allies, the Brits, others that have intelligence, as well as U.S.-owned, SIGINT, human, and other collection.

But I would say the one concern I would have is if people became aware we were primarily taking Syrian refugees from Jordan, there would be an incentive by groups to get their terrorists through Jordan at that point. So, you know, we might be careful in how we publicly discuss that. Thank you.

Mr. KING. Actually my time has expired. But I would just say from listening to the testimony of each of you in answer to the question, there seems to be no real answer here. Because we do have some moral and diplomatic obligation to take some refugees in. But there is really not even close to a reasonable guarantee that we can vet any of them.

Then you have the other issue raised by Dr. Gartenstein-Ross about those who come here and become radicalized. So it would seem no matter how we proceed on this, it just may be a question of trying to minimize the risk. But there is still going to be significant risk there no matter what procedures we follow there, more so than I would say refugees from other countries we have had to deal with in the past so.

With that, I recognize the Ranking Member of the subcommittee, Mr. Higgins.

Mr. HIGGINS. Thank you, Mr. Chairman. I apologize for being late. I was at a meeting on the Iran nuclear negotiations.

Mr. KING. Were you meeting at the White House? Are you name-dropping?

Mr. HIGGINS. No, I didn't say. I apologize. I will ask for unanimous consent to submit my opening statement for the record.

Mr. KING. Yes.

[The statement of Ranking Member Higgins follows:]

STATEMENT OF RANKING MEMBER BRIAN HIGGINS

JUNE 24, 2015

Mr. Chairman, I would like to thank you for holding this hearing to examine the homeland security threat posed by terrorist groups trying to exploit the U.S. Refugee Admissions Program in order to plan or execute terrorist attacks in the United States and abroad. Today, I know we will hear from those who believe this threat is significantly amplified by the influx of Syrian refugees who are expected to be admitted into the United States over the next few years.

While I acknowledge that there have been cases where terrorists, their associates, or foreign nationals have attempted to use the U.S. refugee process as a gateway to facilitate terrorist planning and attacks. However, I would offer that the attempted fraud associated U.S. Refugee program is no more or less than the attempted fraud that exists within other programs. To prevent exploitation, the refugee vetting process has been publicly characterized by a State Department official as "intensive, " "slow," and "rigorous."

Such a process exposes refugees to a great deal of scrutiny from U.S. law enforcement and intelligence agencies. Along with the systems and processes in place, the deliberateness of the process may inherently complicate the timing and ability of terrorists' plans. Throughout our history, the United States has been a haven for refugees fleeing persecution and those who would play on our fears should not derail that proud legacy.

The United States should commit to resettling more of the refugees identified by the U.N. Refugee Agency as needing resettlement. Under our current resettlement plans, the United States is projected to rescue less than 1% of the refugees from Syria. This will not relieve the burden on the other resettlement countries that are hosting millions of refugees and spending billions of dollars on their care.

But it is a first step. I encourage us to find a balance. We must continue to carefully screen refugee applicants for all National security and terrorism concerns. I would urge both my Democratic and Republican colleagues to ensure that sufficient resources and staff are in place and available to ensure that the security vetting process is thorough without hindering resettlement for legitimate refugees.

Prohibiting Syrian refugees from resettlement or lowering the already minimal number of refugees in the United States now, when there is no real evidence that they are a terror threat, would be to actively and explicitly discriminate against them.

Again, I thank Chairman King for his leadership and focusing our oversight on this hearing. However, I would warn us against overstating fears and creating a level of suspicion on an already vulnerable population.

With that, I yield back.

Mr. HIGGINS. Thank you. Thank you. Thank you. The situation in Syria is, obviously, you know, placing extraordinary pressures on Western countries and the United States to accept more refugees from Syria than ever before. So today, you know, how many refugees, Syrian refugees has the United States taken in to date? I would ask each one of the members on the panel.

Mr. GARTENSTEIN-ROSS. The number has been relatively low. I don't have the exact figure on hand. I actually was reading about it this morning. But it is less than the tens of thousands range.

Mr. HIGGINS. Okay.

Mr. FUENTES. That is my understanding, a few thousand. But I don't have the exact numbers.

Mr. JONES. A few thousand again. But I don't have the exact numbers on my fingertips.

Mr. HIGGINS. The United Nations is saying that Syrian refugees, there is about 130,000, that over the next couple of years that will have to go to Western countries and the United States. But the concern, obviously, is the vetting process. That is challenged specifically by not having good intelligence on the ground.

Dr. Jones, you had made reference to Jordan as having the best intelligence. Is that a viable option for the United States and other Western countries to have the vetting process done by Jordanians?

Mr. JONES. I would say in order to protect and maximize U.S. National security, I would never rely on anyone else. I think what would make sense is a layered system. So the Jordanians have a pretty good vetting process. But I think the United States would have to rely on other allies and its own intelligence that it collects by itself.

Mr. HIGGINS. How many U.S. agencies are involved in the vetting process?

Mr. JONES. Well, I think if you are talking about agencies that collect information and pass it, there are, obviously, large numbers in the U.S. Department of Defense, in the U.S. Department of Defense intelligence agencies, in the CIA, in the Department of Homeland Security, and FBI, so a fair number.

Mr. HIGGINS. So one would argue that the current system in place is perhaps a lengthy process but a thorough process?

Mr. JONES. Lengthy process. A thorough process, assuming names get into the system.

Mr. HIGGINS. What is the obstacle to names getting into the system?

Mr. JONES. Well, I think adequate intelligence that, that an individual who is a terrorist or has been facilitating terrorism in a country like Syria has been identified by whether it is the United States or an ally and provided that information. Not just that, but we have the names, the nom de guerres, the spellings of that individual. I mean those are the challenges.

Mr. HIGGINS. Okay. I yield back.

Mr. KING. The gentleman yields back. The gentleman from Pennsylvania, Mr. Barletta.

Mr. BARLETTA. Thank you, Mr. Chairman. In a February hearing before the full House Homeland Security Committee, Assistant Director for the Counterterrorism Division at the FBI Michael Steinbach, commented on the intelligence community's lack of information on the ground in Syria to adequately vet those seeking admission to the United States. He stated that you have to have information to vet.

So the concern in Syria is that we don't have systems in place on the ground to collect the information to vet. Mr. Jones and Mr. Fuentes, based on your experience, how would you assess the intelligence community's ability to obtain the information, necessary to properly screen Syrian refugee applicants for admission? Dr. Jones, do you want to start?

Mr. JONES. Sure. I am not in Government anymore, so I don't have full access to what the United States has in place. But based on my broad understanding of what the United States had in place and has in place in other countries, including Iraq and Afghanistan where it has forces on the ground, that in Syria it has far fewer human collectors, far fewer signals intelligence and other capabilities. So, in that sense, it has much fewer, it has a much weaker ability to collect information that would be useful for the vetting process.

Mr. BARLETTA. Mr. Fuentes.

Mr. FUENTES. Mike Steinbach, the assistant director, worked for me 10 years ago as assistant legal attaché and then later legal attaché in Israel. He is a complete expert in what it takes to gather information from a reliable partner, share intelligence, have cooperation for the mutual security of both sides, the United States and for the country he is working in.

So he knows exactly what the limitations are with Syria when you have no partner, there is no FBI office on the ground in Syria, we have no reliable partner there to gather information from them.

When I say reliable, again, these refugees are going to be basically, they are refugees because they are enemies of the state. So we can't rely on that state to give us good information. Therefore, there is really no source of adequate information to put in any database.

Mr. BARLETTA. Could ISIS and al-Qaeda operatives use our Nation's refugee system to carry out another 9/11-style attack? Is the United States putting itself at risk by accepting refugees from a country where the Government admittedly has insufficient intelligence? Both again.

Mr. JONES. It is possible. It has not generally been their practice to get recruits into the United States through refugee programs. Again, the probability is not zero. But they have generally moved towards trying to inspire people already in the United States through social media and other ways. It is certainly possible though. They have talked about doing this in Syria, Libya, and several other places. But it has not been their main focus.

Mr. FUENTES. In the aftermath of 9/11, the United States, the measures that were taken by U.S. law enforcement, intelligence, DOD, other agencies of the Government, were very extensive and very successful.

The strategy of al-Qaeda at that time was basically, we referred to it in the Bureau as the big bang theory. They wanted the giant, prolific attack that generated world-wide publicity, which 9/11 almost could not be equalled or topped. Other groups that we have seen over the years, Hezbollah, Hamas, and others, believed in a different philosophy, death by a thousand cuts.

So they were willing to do a bombing at a bus station in Israel or at a discotheque or in a cafeteria, kill four or five people at a time, maybe 50 people on a bus. But they were happy with that because they were also killing people that were engaged in everyday life which meant the whole population thought wait a minute, I take a bus, I go to school, I go to a cafeteria and eat, that could be me. So that generated terror at a different level. Over the years, because we have tracked international financing, the fact that Osama bin Laden would not have been able to exert command and control like he did on the 9/11 attack, personally meeting and vetting each of the hijackers, approving the individuals submitted to him by Khalid Sheikh Mohammed, you can't exercise that kind of control over an attack by courier or remote control where you are not in communication.

Communication is essential to fight them. It is essential for them to carry out the attack. That is what was eliminated. So in this situation, you know, we have a situation where I don't think any Syrian refugee through that process, not any Syrian but a Syrian refugee through this process is going to be able to come in and mastermind a 9/11. Can they come in and do the street corner attack, run over people, stab people, you know, the death by a thousand cuts, in some cases literally, yes. But any terrorist and any radicalized American, we are seeing that every day with arrests by the FBI for people willing to do so that type of attack and the difficulty in stopping that.

Mr. BARLETTA. Thank you. Thank you, Mr. Chairman.

Mr. KING. The gentleman yields back. The gentleman from Texas, Mr. Vela.

Mr. VELA. Dr. Jones, obviously, the challenges of intelligence gathering in Syria are great. You started to talk about our relationship with Jordan and what they are doing on that end. I was wondering if you could elaborate on our relationship with Jordan. Also, after Jordan, what are the other countries that we should be looking at in terms of this kind of information sharing?

Mr. JONES. So the U.S. relationship with Jordan has, obviously, been long-standing. There is, my understanding, a training going on with Jordan with rebels operating in Syria. So there is, there has been intelligence sharing between the United States and Jordan about individuals that are being trained to fight against the Assad regime or actually as the administration argues against the Islamic State in Syria.

There have been concerns about weapons of mass destruction in Syria. So the Jordanians and the Americans have worked fairly closely on building the capability to go in and seize weapons of mass destruction if they were to be found, additional ones were to be found in Syria. So the relationship is fairly robust between the United States and Jordan. Where I would have concerns is some of the other countries in the region.

Lebanon has got a fairly weak government, has historically had one. Hezbollah contains to play an important role in the political system in Lebanon. Probably not as good of a way to vet through Lebanon. Iraq, I have little faith that the Iraqi Government will be helpful in vetting. It has had a hard time controlling its own territory from ISIS.

Then Turkey, Turkey is a NATO country. It certainly has an ability to monitor but Turkey has had a very difficult time managing the foreign fighter route through its own country. So Turkey's ability is circumspect to some degree. It is the predominant pipeline, if you need to get to Syria, to get there, you go through Turkey. So, again, I have concerns about Turkey's ability, though it is a NATO country, to keep a close eye on that.

Mr. VELA. So from the Syrian refugee standpoint, are those four countries basically the first stop?

Mr. JONES. Yes. They are the largest, as far as I am aware, they are the largest locations for Syrian refugees, yes.

Mr. VELA. Now, is there anything else you think we need to do in terms of enhancing our relationship with Jordan?

Mr. JONES. In addition to continuing to provide intelligence sharing between the United States and Jordan, nothing off the top of my head, no.

I think the biggest challenge the United States is going to have is probably in Turkey, in Lebanon, and then in Iraq where its fidelity on the intelligence is just weaker.

Mr. VELA. I guess this is a question for both you and Mr. Fuentes. From the standpoint of intelligence gathering overall in Syria, what else do you think we can do? I mean, is it a resource issue or——

Mr. FUENTES. I think with Syria, it is not a resource issue. We have to have a stable government there. We have to have, I think we are not going be able to do this until we have the aftermath of whatever is happening now and some government is in control of that whole country and, hopefully, becomes a partner of the United States.

Now, we could have what we have in Libya where you just have chaos and a failed state. That could occur. Or we could have dual states there of the Assad regime controlling maybe Damascus and part of the country, and ISIS or other groups, al-Nusra, the other part of the country. So it is going to be difficult for us to have a working partner there at any level and a partner that we can trust their information if they give it to us.

When you asked about Amman, I mean, about Jordan, the United States has had a tremendous relationship all through, you know, before the Iraq war, during the Iraq war, they served as basically a base for us to go from, as did Kuwait at that time. But also the Jordanians for us built a giant police academy just outside of Amman so that Iraqi police officers could be vetted by U.S. agencies, brought to that location by the thousands, and trained and then returned back to Iraq.

You have noticed, we haven't had the issue in Iraq over the years of police officers and Iraqis killing Americans like we later faced in Afghanistan on several occasions. So that program was successful. Also when the process of, as I mentioned, I opened the FBI's office, the formal attaché office in Baghdad in 2004. At that time, it was decided that that embassy was going to be either the largest or second-largest embassy in the U.S. system. The largest being Cairo, Egypt.

So they were expecting about 1,000 people to be employed in the service of that embassy. Jordan volunteered that the United States could have a second partial embassy of Baghdad based in Amman where it would be safer and, therefore, not need 1,000 people in Baghdad to service the Iraqi-Baghdad legal—I mean Embassy at the time. So they have been tremendously helpful. Their partnership has been strong. The cross-training that has gone on between their personnel and American personnel has been outstanding.

So I don't know that we could increase, you know, it is hard to be a stronger partner with them. We have certain partners like that in the world that you wonder how you could be closer, whether it is Israel or whether it is the British or the Australians. But, you know, the situation is what are they able to get from Syria, can they do any better than we can? I think at the moment, it is questionable that they can.

Mr. VELA. Thank you. I yield back.

Mr. KING. The gentleman yields back.

I would just add I don't know of any closer ally we have in the world than Jordan, I mean, at every level of cooperation of Jordan is first class, of Jordanians is first class.

I received five statements for the record from non-profit groups that work with refugees. I ask unanimous consent that they be included in the record. Without objection.

[The information follows:]

STATEMENT OF HIAS

JUNE 24, 2015

Throughout our history, America has been defined by our generosity toward those who seek a safe haven from oppression. An asylum system that is fair, effective, and humane honors both our country's history and reflects the deeply-held American and Jewish tradition of offering a chance at a new beginning to those who seek safety and freedom. Once given that opportunity, refugees and asylees become active and productive members of American communities.

In the aftermath of World War II, when the price for keeping doors closed to refugees was made starkly clear, the international community adopted the 1951 United Nations Convention relating to the Status of Refugees, which to this day defines who is a refugee and what legal protection a refugee is entitled to receive and is the basis for the U.S. refugee and asylum law.

The Immigration and Nationality Act provides a way for those fleeing persecution to seek refuge while preventing those who pose a threat or danger to the United States from entering. The law established mechanisms to screen for potential threats. The procedure for screening out applicants for refugee status that may pose a threat to the United States has only become more rigorous since September 11. Today the refugee program has the most thorough security screenings of any form of immigration relief.

Refugee applicants undergo multiple security screenings at almost every step of the process of resettlement to the United States. The Department of State and the Department of Homeland Security share in the responsibility of screening refugee applicants. An applicant's biographic information and biometric information are vetted against multiple law enforcement and intelligence databases including the State Department's Consular Lookout and Support System (CLASS), which includes the Government's terrorist watch list information, the Federal Bureau of Investigation (FBI) Integrated Automated Fingerprint Identification System (IAFIS), and DHS's Automated Biometric Identification System (IDENT). This is in addition to the in-person interview conducted by DHS staff to ascertain the validity of the claim for refugee status.

HIAS believes that National security and assistance to refugees from Syria are not incompatible. Syrian refugees are subject to the rigorous security screening processes in place. Many of those seeking asylum are victims of terrorism and are trying to find safety from extremism. The U.S. refugee program can offer them that safety and still protect the United States from possible threats.

There are some Syrian refugees who will never be able to return home or live safely a country of first asylum. The United States can help the countries of first asylum that have shouldered the responsibility for so many Syrians fleeing the crisis by providing assistance and resettling some of the most vulnerable refugees who are unable to live in these countries in safety. By doing so, the United States will proudly honor its tradition of providing safe haven for refugees and ensure that the most vulnerable can rebuild their shattered lives free of fear.

STATEMENT OF SYRIAN COMMUNITY NETWORK (CHICAGO, IL), SYRIAN AMERICAN MEDICAL SOCIETY, KARAM FOUNDATION, SYRIA RELIEF AND DEVELOPMENT, SYRIAN EXPATRIATES ORGANIZATION, WATAN USA, RAHMA RELIEF FOUNDATION, HOPE FOR SYRIA

JUNE 24, 2015

Dear Chairman Peter King, Ranking Member Brian Higgins, and Members of the Subcommittee: We write to you as a group of non-political Syrian American-led humanitarian organizations that provide multi-sector relief inside of Syria, to refugees and host countries in the region, and to Syrian refugees in the United States. Our efforts together help millions of Syrians, both those who remain in Syria and those displaced as refugees. Our programs cover the full range of humanitarian sectors, including community services, education, food and non-food items, health, protection, water/sanitation/hygiene, and women's empowerment. In addition to emergency relief, our organizations have established development projects that promote sustainable living and lay the groundwork for voluntary refugee return, such as building schools, facilitating jobs and skills training, and helping to establish bakeries and flour mills. Together, we support over 100 health facilities and almost 1,000 medical staff inside of Syria who operate under the principle of medical neutrality and risk their lives to save others. Our organizations prioritize education, psychosocial support, and community healing. We've been fortunate to have leading

Congressional officials visit our field programs to see their impact on Syrian refugees, and we've had the opportunity to advocate for humanitarian support for Syria and Syrian refugees at the highest levels of U.S. Government, from President Obama to Secretary Jeh Johnson to leaders of the House and Senate.

We further represent a constituency of Syrian Americans, humanitarian allies, and local volunteers throughout the United States, from Texas to New York. As the crisis has become increasingly protracted, our organizations have begun to work with local resettled Syrian refugees in the United States, coordinating with volunteers, refugee agencies, and civic and religious organizations to ensure that Syrian refugees are welcomed and assisted in their transition. Our built-in networks of Syrian American and partner communities have been invaluable in these transitions.

We are humbled to submit this statement to the House Homeland Security Subcommittee on Counterterrorism and Intelligence on admitting Syrian refugees. As you know, the United Nations estimates that about 4 million people have fled Syria and 7.6 million others are internally displaced. Over 230,000 Syrians have been killed since 2011. As Mr. António Guterres, the United Nations High Commissioner for Refugees, said recently: ''The Syrian war unleashed the worst humanitarian crisis of our time.''

The enormous flow of refugees has created a strain on host countries in the region, which are forced to deal with extreme economic pressures, overcrowded hospitals, shortages of basic public services, and growing resentment among host communities. The regional dynamics of Lebanon, Jordan, and Turkey, which have taken on the majority of the refugee burden, have been altered over the last few years. The conflict in Syria has led to a regional crisis, and the sheer numbers of refugees and lack of support for host communities threaten the stability of these countries. However, as Anne Richard, the Assistant Secretary for the Bureau of Population, Refugees, and Migration at the Department of State, said: '' . . . These very real burdens must pale in comparison to the daily struggles of Syrians themselves. Imagine losing practically everything—your loved ones, your home, your profession, and your dignity.''

We commend the United States Government for taking a leadership role to stand for these vulnerable refugees and to offer them a glimpse of hope. Throughout history, the United States has always taken a leadership role in assisting vulnerable refugees. The United States has accepted the majority of all UNHCR referrals from around the world. In 2013, United States reached its goal of resettling nearly 70,000 refugees from nearly 70 countries. Now, the United States has put forth invaluable efforts to resettle vulnerable Syrian refugees.

We have worked closely with our partners at the U.S. Refugee Admissions Program, coordinated by the Bureau of Population, Refugees, and Migration at the Department of State and the Department of Homeland Security, along the way. We commend their meticulous and exemplary work. All Syrian refugee profiles being actively considered for resettlement are reviewed thoroughly by the U.S. Refugee Admissions Program with support and leadership from the White House and security vetting agencies. These Syrians go through extensive security background checks. The majority of Syrian refugees being considered for resettlement are among the most vulnerable populations of women and children seeking to flee the effects of conflict. With assistance from the International Organization for Migration, they are provided with medical exams and logistics for transportation before coming to the United States.

Once Syrian refugees arrive, our groups work alongside a network of resettlement agencies, non-profits, churches and mosques, civic organizations, and local volunteers to welcome them. These U.S. groups work in 180 communities across the country to ensure refugees have access to work, education, opportunities to improve their English, and what they and their families need to be comfortable and have a happy and healthy future.

The Syrian Community Network is a prime example of a volunteer-led organization working closely with resettled Syrian families to ease their transition, focusing particularly on the Chicago area. The Syrian Community Network works with 10 families that have been resettled through various agencies. One family in particular stands out as an upcoming success story. Resettled in Chicago in January 2015, Mayada is a single mother with 6 children ranging between the ages of 4 and 19. Her two oldest children, Zeyd and Zeynab, hold steady jobs and help to pay rent, all while they attend ESL classes at the local community college. The four younger children—Wedad, Zakaria, Shahed, and Shaima—have been performing remarkably in school, exceeding expectations. They all dream of graduating college and becoming doctors, teachers, computer engineers, and so much more. The youngest daughter, Shaima, decided that she wants to be a photojournalist after a Chicago journalist interviewed her. Just recently, Wedad, who will be in ninth grade in the fall, was accepted into the "GirlForward" summer program designed for bright adolescent refugee girls in the city of Chicago. Syrians are known to have an entrepreneurial spirit and, given the opportunity, Syrian refugees will become the next American success story.

We strongly urge the Homeland Security Subcommittee on Counterterrorism and Intelligence to support their counterparts at the Department of State and Department of Homeland Security as they work to further increase resettlement numbers for vulnerable Syrian refugees in 2015 and beyond. The families and individuals being considered for resettlement face dire protection challenges and often need specialized care. Among those being considered are victims of torture, women at risk, persons with disabilities, LGBTQ persons facing risk, women-headed households, and those facing acute security threats. To prohibit Syrian refugees from the option of U.S. resettlement because of the presence of ISIL and other extremist groups in Syria, and not based on thorough U.S.-led security checks and humanitarian needs assessments, discounts the commendable work of the Department of Homeland Security and Department of State and amounts to blatant discrimination based on nationality. The Homeland Security Subcommittee on Counterterrorism and Intelligence should work to further ensure sufficient staffing and capacity for security vetting agencies to increase their ability to conduct thorough and quick security checks.

Our organizations function as implementing partners for many of the major INGOs and U.N. agencies in Syria and coordinate with the U.S. agencies taking the lead refugee resettlement here at home. Our talented staff and volunteers have been the backbone of crisis relief for Syria and have a comprehensive understanding of the changing situation on the ground. From seeing the trends of displacement in Syria and the region first-hand, we think that it is essential for the United States to take a leading role in Syrian refugee resettlement for the protection of Syria's vulnerable refugees, for the stability and security of the region, and for the relevance of the United States as a humanitarian and global leader. We strongly encourage the Homeland Security Subcommittee on Counterterrorism and Intelligence to work with relevant U.S. departments and the administration to ensure that vulnerable Syrian refugees continue to have the hope of resettlement and a brighter future.

––––––––

STATEMENT OF MIRNA BARQ, PRESIDENT, SYRIAN AMERICAN COUNCIL

MAY 21, 2015

Chairman King, Ranking Member Higgins, and Members of the subcommittee: The Syrian American Council is the largest and oldest Syrian American community organization in the United States. Founded in 2005 in Burr Ridge, Illinois, SAC is a multi-ethnic, multi-confessional, non-partisan organization that incorporates all segments of the Syrian American community. Our activities include community organizing, youth empowerment, media outreach, advocacy, and support for pro-democracy activists in Syria. SAC has 23 local chapters Nation-wide.

SAC is honored to submit this statement for the record to the Subcommittee on Counterterrorism and Intelligence. Significant communities of Syrian Americans exist in many areas of the United States, including New York, Texas, Iowa, Florida, Ohio, Pennsylvania, Michigan, and Ohio. Their income levels are above the median for American citizens and many of them provide jobs and livelihoods for other Americans in their locale. Older community members have found in America a democratic haven from political persecution, while our youth have grown up here and consider American culture their own.

As a young Christian growing up in Damascus, I personally was blessed to have experienced the wonders and beauty of the holiday season in my beloved Syria. The memories of festivities throughout the Damascus old city, the carolers, the beautifully lit Christmas trees, the nativity mangers, and the churches filled with celebrants will stay with me forever. Each year, I take the time to describe my experience to friends and family in my hometown of Orlando, Florida so they will understand the inherent tolerance and diversity of the Syrian people. That inherent tolerance and diversity is now under attack.

The Syrian American community shares your dismay at the rise of the so-called Islamic State of Iraq and Syria (ISIS) and at the urgent home-grown terror threat that has resulted from this rise. We are also painfully aware that ISIS has exploited the crisis in Syria to turn our ancestral homeland into a locus for recruitment. ISIS has severely impeded our ability to get help to ordinary Syrians in need. At times,

Syrian Americans have been forced into hasty exits from their humanitarian work inside Syria after finding out that ISIS had marked them for death.

We consider ISIS our enemies, and as such, we are keen to help Congress and the U.S. Government as they work to stop these extremists. SAC has already partnered with the Office for Civil Rights and Civil Liberties at the Department of Homeland Security to organize community briefings for Syrian Americans. In addition, staff members of the SAC have briefed senior White House officials on ISIS activities inside Syria. We encourage a robust Congressional debate on how ISIS can be stopped both at home and abroad.

Along these lines, it is important to note that Syrian immigrants to the United States are in no way the leading demographic of foreign fighters joining ISIS. Out of over 150 U.S. nationals who have successfully joined or attempted to join ISIS in Syria and Iraq, we know of only one potential case involving a Syrian American (who is not charged with having joined ISIS). By contrast, many U.S.-born citizens have joined ISIS, including citizens with no ancestry from majority-Muslim countries. Clearly, barring vulnerable Syrian refugees from entering America will not address this vast majority of cases.

America is a Nation of immigrants and always has been. Each year, the United States admits some 70,000 refugees as new citizens, and the Syrian refugee crisis is far and away the worst refugee crisis in the world today. United Nations High Commissioner for Refugees Antonio Guterres has referred to the Syrian refugee crisis as ''the worst humanitarian disaster since the end of the Cold War.'' Furthermore, the majority of Syrian refugees up for resettlement are not fighting-age males, but innocent women and children seeking to flee the vicious conflict. They live in horrible conditions, and every winter, multiple child refugees die for lack of heating and winter clothing. Many refugees even have family members or close friends and associates within the Syrian American community who are ready to care for them.

To bar Syrian refugees from resettlement in the United States now, when their need is so great and when there is no real evidence that they are a terror threat, would be to actively and explicitly discriminate against them—against us—simply for being Syrian. We as Syrian Americans encourage our Congress Members to support the fight against ISIS and defend our country against home-grown terrorism without contributing to the demonization of the entire Syrian community.

Founded in 2005 in Burr Ridge, Illinois, the Syrian American Council is the largest Syrian-American community organization in the United States. It serves to amplify the voice of the Syrian-American Community. SAC is a multi-ethnic, multi-confessional, non-partisan organization that includes members from all segments of Syrian society, and has over 23 chapters Nation-wide. It is an organization devoted to community organizing, awareness-raising, youth empowerment, media outreach, advocacy, and support for Syrians seeking to build a free and democratic Syria.

STATEMENT OF LUTHERAN IMMIGRATION AND REFUGEE SERVICE

JUNE 24, 2015

Lutheran Immigration and Refugee Service (LIRS) appreciates the opportunity to submit its views on the United States Refugee Admissions Program as it pertains to Syrian refugees. As the national organization founded by Lutherans to serve uprooted people, LIRS is committed to helping those who have been forced to flee their homes find protection. Following God's call in scripture to uphold justice for the sojourner, LIRS serves as a leader in calling for the protection of vulnerable migrants and refugees, including children and families from Syria.

For over 75 years, LIRS has worked to welcome over 400,000 refugees to the United States on behalf of the Evangelical Lutheran Church in America, the Lutheran Church—Missouri Synod and the Latvian Evangelical Lutheran Church in America. In fiscal year 2014, LIRS and its Refugee Resettlement affiliates welcomed over 11,000 refugees to their new communities and empowered them to build new lives.

Resettlement in a third country is considered a durable solution and a last resort for only a small fraction of the world's most vulnerable refugees. LIRS is proud to be one of nine agencies that partners with the Federal Government, particularly the Department of State's Bureau of Population, Refugees, and Migration (PRM) and the Department of Health and Human Services' Office of Refugee Resettlement (ORR) to be a part of this solution. LIRS is dismayed that despite the United Nations High Commissioner for Refugees (UNHCR) registering over 4 million Syrian refugees, half of whom are children, only a precious few Syrian refugees have been resettled in the United States.

The United States Refugee Admissions Program (USRAP) located within the Department of Homeland Security (DHS), U.S. Citizenship and Immigration Services (USCIS) agency continually achieves its dual mission to offer resettlement opportunities to eligible refugees while safeguarding the integrity of the program and the United States National security. To protect U.S. National security, DHS provides advanced training to its refugee adjudicators on security protocols, fraud detention, and fraud prevention. In addition, each refugee considered for resettlement in the United States goes through a multi-layered screening process before coming to the United States. These processes include multiple biographic and biometric checks by U.S. security vetting agencies which are routinely updated, in-person interviews with trained adjudication's officers and ''pre-departure'' checks. No case is finally approved until results from all security checks have been received and analyzed.

To add unnecessary security screening mechanisms to this already robust process would needlessly harm individuals who need protection by delaying their resettlement. ''Sadly, the Syrian refugee population includes severely vulnerable individuals: Women and girls at risk, survivors of torture and violence, and persons with serious medical needs or disabilities,'' said Linda Hartke, LIRS president and CEO. ''LIRS and our national network stand ready to do what it takes to welcome into U.S. communities the most vulnerable Syrian refugees who cannot return home or integrate in the countries currently hosting them.''

The U.S. Refugee Admissions Program offers refugees safe haven and a chance at a new life, while also bringing tangible benefits to the communities that welcome them. Having endured incredible hardship and unimaginable horrors in their home countries, refugees often spend years exiled in host countries once they flee, awaiting the opportunity to rebuild their lives. In the case of Syrian refugees, host countries in the region are increasingly strained and unable to offer benefits or stability. Once they are resettled in a third country, refugees routinely become engaged and productive community members, contributing economically, socially, and spiritually to our communities. The support of welcoming communities, congregations, volunteers, employers, schools, foster families, and others makes resettlement a successful public-private partnership. The Federal Government, particularly PRM and ORR, and State governments play a vital role.

The conflict in Syria only continues to worsen. As mentioned, UNHCR has registered over 4 million refugees, half of whom are children, who have been forced to flee to neighboring countries. It is LIRS's position that the United States should commit to resettling a higher number of vulnerable Syrian refugees. However, to achieve this goal, more focus and resources must be committed to the admission process as well as the resettlement and integration of newly-arriving refugees.

INCREASED FUNDING NEEDS AND NECESSARY RESETTLEMENT REFORMS

Resources available to refugee families and adults through ORR have remained stagnant for many years. To ensure that Syrian refugees resettled in the United States would receive the help they need to locate housing, receive medical attention and employment assistance, among other services, and to promote self-sufficiency and long-term integration this funding must be increased. While private support plays an important role in the reception and integration of refugees, Federal resources are critical to ensure refugees receive essential services. Refugee populations arriving to the United States have changed significantly since the formal establishment of the resettlement program in the Refugee Act of 1980. Today's refugee population is much more diverse and vulnerable than it was more than three decades ago. However, services lack flexibility to be responsive to the diverse strengths and needs of refugees arriving today. Furthermore, ORR's mandate has expanded over the years from serving resettled refugees to include asylees, Iraqi and Afghan Special Immigrant Visa recipients, Cuban and Haitian entrants, survivors of human trafficking and torture and unaccompanied children. Because funding has not kept up with these changes in ORR's mandate and diversifying client needs, ORR has strained to provide sufficient support and services to all of the populations under its care.

REFORMS TO TERRORISM-RELATED INADMISSIBILITY GROUNDS

Under immigration law, an individual cannot be admitted to the United States if they have provided material support, including insignificant material support, to an undesignated terrorist organization; a member of such an organization; or to an individual the individual knows, or reasonably should know, has committed or plans to commit a terrorist activity. In 2001, Congress enacted legislation that significantly broadened the definition of ''terrorist activity.''

As a result, refugees, including many vulnerable Syrian refugees, who pose no threat to National security face denial of protection and resettlement in the United States due to unintended consequences of the overly-broad application of the "material support to terrorist organizations" bar (and related bars) to admission. Indeed, current law threatens to exclude any Syrians who fought with any armed opposition group in Syria (regardless of whether or not the individual applicant was involved in any violations of international humanitarian law or other crimes), anyone who provided "material support" to any opposition force or opposition fighter, anyone who solicited funds or members for such a force, and even anyone whose spouse or parent is found to have done these things.

These bars are duplicative and carry severe consequences. As mentioned previously, refugees are required to pass intense security screenings and background checks as part of the admission process. People who commit war crimes, crimes against humanity, or who persecute others are inadmissible to the United States under other provisions of our immigration laws. However, overly broad "terrorism" bars prevent the ability of the United States to provide welcome to bona fide refugees seeking safety.

LIRS RECOMMENDATIONS

LIRS's expertise, experience, and compassion—drawn from decades of welcoming vulnerable newcomers—inspires our advocacy. To address current resettlement needs facing refugees, including millions of Syrian refugees, and improve welcome for refugees in the United States, LIRS makes the following recommendations to Congress:

- Ensure robust funding of the Department of State's Bureau of Population, Refugees, and Migration and the Department of Health and Human Services' Office of Refugee Resettlement to better protect and assist refugees overseas and those resettled to the United States.
- Enact pending legislation to strengthen refugee protections and resettlement, including the bi-partisan Protecting Religious Minorities Persecuted by ISIS Act of 2015 (H.R. 1568).
- Amend problematic anti-terrorism provisions that define "material support" too broadly.
- Increase the Presidential Determination from 70,000 refugees in fiscal year 2015 to 100,000 refugees in fiscal year 2016 to allow resettlement of Syrian refugees in addition to on-going resettlement of other refugees from around the world.

If you have any questions about this statement, please contact Brittney Nystrom, LIRS Director for Advocacy.

————

STATEMENT OF CWS, CHURCH WORLD SERVICE

JUNE 24, 2015

Church World Service, a 69-year-old humanitarian organization representing 37 Christian denominations, works to assist refugees through protection internationally and by providing resettlement services to help refugees adjust to their new lives and integrate in the United States.

The U.S. Refugee Admissions Program is a life-saving, public-private partnership that helps rescue refugees who have no other means of finding safety. To be considered a refugee, individuals must prove that they have fled persecution due to their nationality, ethnicity, religion, political opinion, or membership in a particular social group. Refugees face three options: Return to their home country, integrate in the country to which they first fled, or be resettled to a third country. For the millions who are unable to return home due to significant threats to their safety and are rejected by the country to which they first fled, resettlement is the last resort. While less than 1 percent of the world's estimated 15 million refugees are resettled to a third country, resettlement saves lives and also helps encourage other countries to provide durable solutions for refugees within their borders, including local integration. The United States has a long history of providing protection to persons fleeing persecution, and U.S. communities, schools, congregations, and employers welcome refugees and help them integrate in their new homes. In turn, refugees contribute to their new communities with their innovative skills, dedicated work, and inspiring perseverance.

Currently, Syria is experiencing the worst humanitarian crisis the world has seen in 20 years, with approximately 4 million refugees who have fled the country and 7.6 million internally displaced. Roughly three-quarters of those displaced are women and children. Lebanon, Jordan, Turkey, Iraq, and Egypt currently host more than 3.9 million registered Syrian refugees and thousands more who are not registered. Specifically, religious minorities living in ISIS-held territories, including Christians, Yezidids, Shabaks, Turkoman Shiites, Coptic Christians, Druze, Mandeans and Assyrians have fled in the thousands. While this crisis is complex and requires a variety of solutions, refugee resettlement plays a strategic role in alleviating pressure on host countries in the region, galvanizing international awareness of the human costs of the crisis, and providing durable solutions and opportunities for a new life for vulnerable populations fleeing persecution. Many European countries have welcomed Syrians through resettlement and humanitarian admissions schemes, including Germany pledging to accept 30,000; Sweden to resettle 2,700 and with more than 9,000 asylum applications pending; and Norway, France, Austria, Finland, and other countries working to provide protection and resettlement to Syrian refugees. While traditionally a world leader in refugee resettlement, the United States has resettled only a small numbers of Syrian refugees.

The refugee resettlement program is the most difficult way to enter the United States, routinely taking individuals referred to the program longer than 1,000 days to be processed. Security measures are intrinsic to the integrity of the refugee program, and over the years, the U.S. Government has continuously fine-tuned the system to maximize domestic security. All refugees undergo thorough and rigorous security screenings prior to arriving to the United States, including but not limited to multiple biographic and identity investigations; FBI biometric checks of applicants' fingerprints and photographs; in-depth, in-person interviews by well-trained Department of Homeland Security officers; medical screenings; and other checks by U.S. domestic and international intelligence agencies, including additional biographical screening by the National Counterterrorism Center (NCTC) since August 2011. *www.rcusa.org/uploads/pdfs/How\Refugees\Get\to\the\US\Chart.pdf.* In addition, mandatory supervisory review of all decisions; random case assignment; inter-agency National security teams; trained document experts; forensic testing of documents; and interpreter monitoring are important checks in place to maintain the security of the refugee resettlement program.

CWS urges the United States to welcome refugees and asylum seekers impacted by the Syrian conflict and ensure access to resettlement by the most vulnerable Syrian refugees, with special attention to women and girls, children in adversity, and other highly vulnerable populations. CWS stands committed to working with both chambers of Congress and the administration to resettle Syrian refugees as part of our foreign policy interests and humanitarian responsibilities. We urge all Members of Congress to support these efforts to provide safety to vulnerable refugees from Syria and beyond.

Mr. KING. Now, the gentleman from New York, Mr. Katko.

Mr. KATKO. Thank you. I want to echo the sentiments of the Chairman that there is a moral imperative to try and do something to help these refugees. There is no question about that. I had the good fortune with the task force that I am part of to go to the Middle East and see first-hand the gravity of the situation in Baghdad and flying over Jordan and seeing the camps and in Turkey, as well as in many other places.

So, yeah, we do have a moral imperative; but we also have a duty as leaders of this great Nation to protect our citizens. That therein lies the rub, I guess, right? So, I want to analyze this a little bit in a bifurcated manner and first just ask you each a simple question. Do any of you think it is a good idea to allow refugees into this country when you can't properly vet them? Forget about the moral side of it. Just answer me; from a security standpoint, is it a good idea? Does anybody think it is? No. I think we are unanimous in that. Am I right?

Okay. So then the question then becomes, what do you do? Can we help them somehow in other ways, other than bringing them here? Is that something that anyone has contemplated, and if they have, how can we do that? I would like to hear from each of you on that.

Mr. GARTENSTEIN-ROSS. I agree with that, and I think that looking at this through a National interest perspective is important. At the end of the day as American policymakers, there is a strong duty, obviously, to the American public.

Actually addressing the situation over there, is I think, very important and arguably may get more bang for the buck because if you look at the percentage, you know, right now we are looking at taking in 70,000 refugees this year of which about 33,000 would be from the region, so the maximum is about 33- to 35,000 Syrian refugees. That is a drop in the bucket.

If you look at the situation on the ground in the camps, trying to improve the situation in the camps, providing job opportunities, educational opportunities, often people who are in camps are set back significantly in their education, particularly because as the populations initially went there, they thought that they would be there temporarily; and so children ended up missing a year or more equivalent of school in addition to the situation that is there.

The one thing I would point to that I would be cautious of is that, particularly in Jordan, since most of the refugees there are not in camps, there is a great deal of tension between the native Jordanian population and the refugees; and so any sort of jobs program that is aimed specifically at refugees may generate more resentment. But I think thinking about that angle and what you can for the region, is both from a security perspective and probably from a domestic resource perspective, has advantages and may actually be from kind of the overall humanitarian perspective, the best use of our money.

Mr. KATKO. Thank you very much. Mr. Fuentes.

Mr. FUENTES. Yes, I would agree with that. If you provide the type of resources that maybe make these camps more livable, make them, you know, better in terms of humanitarian cause, not just care and feeding and shelter, but also educational programs and other opportunities, the length of time that you would be providing those services would also be a deterrent to terrorists because they wouldn't want to take the time to have to have somebody go through a 1- or 2-year program to go through that process.

Then they would have to worry that they would lose them, that they would become pro-United States or pro-West as opposed to whatever cause they thought they were sending them to. So I think that if we did more for the refugees before they got here and it took a longer time to do that, it might in itself be a deterrent.

Mr. KATKO. Dr. Jones.

Mr. JONES. I think a range of those steps would be helpful. I would have two additional comments. One is I think a long-term strategy for Syria right now is lacking, and I think in addition to refugee issues, finding ways to wind down the war through political, military, and other steps would be useful. I don't believe we have a long-term strategy at the moment, and I would urge whatever administration comes next as well as this one to make this a priority based on the threats that we are talking about.

The other issue I would just note is I think we have got these vetting challenges in a range of countries we are now seeing extremists; Libya, Afghanistan, Pakistan, Yemen, Somalia, Iraq. The Islamic State has expanded into a range of these countries. So, again, I would also note that this vetting issue is problematic in a number of them, and even in the Yemen case our presence there has declined significantly over the last several years, including our intelligence picture. So we have got this problem in several places.

Mr. KATKO. Yeah. I am glad to hear you all pretty much agree with what I believe to be the issue is; we can't have people coming into this country where we can't properly vet them. Especially in this day and age where ISIS is trying different ways to probe and get in here as well.

So, I think maybe taking a fresher look at what we can do while they are still over there is something which might fulfill the moral imperative we have to help them, and that is something we should probably think about a little bit more and talk about a little more fully going forward. So thank you, gentleman.

Mr. KING. The gentleman from Massachusetts, Mr. Keating.

Mr. KEATING. Thank you, Mr. Chairman. Getting back to our own intelligence in Syria, we talked about what we can gain from other countries. Now since we have had limited, you know, people on the ground there, how much has it improved our own internal intelligence on Syria? Any idea? It had to have gotten better because it was at a very low ebb.

Mr. JONES. My assessment is if you look at the U.S. intelligence and military's targeting in Syria, including of Khorasan targets, it is obviously good enough to take out some very serious al-Qaeda, al-Nusrah, and some Islamic State targets, so I think the capability is better today than it was a year or 2 ago. So better. That doesn't mean good.

Mr. KEATING. We have had witnesses at other hearings in other committees testify that Assad's position is much more precarious than it was.

How would you speculate things might change in terms of the refugee situation if he is gone, if he is out of power personally, you know, whether or not he is replaced by someone more or less aligned to his own administration or someone else? I know it is speculative, but how significant would that be, given the fact that I do believe that he is in a much more precarious situation.

Mr. FUENTES. I think it would depend on who he is replaced with. If we have ISIS take over the whole country or Khorasan Group or other al-Qaeda affiliates, we have gone from bad to worse, but actually it is bad already. So I think that the intelligence assets that we do have on the ground in Syria right now to help target who we want to get in terms of members of adversarial groups is one thing.

To have them be in a position to vet refugees, they are not going to be able to do that. They are in a covert, very dangerous, precarious situation. So I think that is a different ability for our intelligence services.

Mr. KEATING. The same people testified, just for the record, you know, that it would be highly unlikely, you know, that it would be one of those groups that would be able to take over in that kind of change.

Dr. Jones had a comment with the Visa Waiver Program, how we should be more engaged in that. Clearly there is a concern that if people resettle and they are there and there is a lower level of security, how do you propose we better engage with that program, the Visa Waiver Program?

Mr. JONES. I think part of this is continuing to work with European allies. I think some of that has improved over the last year or two in getting names on lists. The Germans have been more cooperative in providing names of individuals they have been concerned about. So I think part of the issue on Visa Waiver is continuing to get more granular information on names of individuals of concern for terrorist activity. Different spellings of names, noms de guerre. That is the direction I would encourage on Visa Waiver.

Mr. KEATING. The other question I have, of the small number of refugees we have in the United States now, how is that broken down with women and children? Any figures in that respect? Any estimates in that respect at all? None.

Well, the other issue really is one in the larger sense of our allies. You have referenced, you know, one country, Germany, that is vetting this as well. I was a part of the same group that went through not only through the Mideast, but through Europe, looking at any pathways for foreign fighters. But I think the same thing can be said, too, in terms of the concern with the refugees in Turkey, 1.9 million, they told us, refugees are there. They have 40 million people coming in and out of the Istanbul Airport, largely with people leaving there, having no information provided to us.

When you mentioned how there is a disparity among some of our allied countries in Europe, can you name some of the things that should be done, and particularly what countries could use more engagement on our part?

Mr. FUENTES. I think in terms of international cooperation, you know, we do have outstanding relationships with our European allies and almost all of the Middle East countries where we have a partner relationship. Some places we don't have it.

I mentioned that I served as a member of the Executive Committee of Interpol, and many of these countries are also, including Iran, members of Interpol. So there is some dialogue even in those channels that we often can use in spite of the public stance that a country might be our enemy, you know, back channel, we do on occasion get some help from a number of these countries if they see the same threat to them that we see to us. That becomes the issue here.

In terms of Germany, there is a large Turkish population in Germany, so they have had some degree of success in getting cooperation, having sources of information, from the Turkish population; and the Germans have been very welcoming of the immigrant population from Turkey that has come there and now in some cases, you know the other groups that come there also.

But our European allies again, many of these countries are underresourced in terms of these kind of threats, and the Visa Waiver Program does give an opportunity. I know Director Mueller over the time when he was director of the FBI repeatedly testified that he opposed the Waiver Program because of the ease of access or the easier access for individuals if they were radicalized in Europe that have European passports that could come here.

That being said, there was no intention ever of changing that policy based on the business between Europe and the United States and the complete other concerns of interaction that we have that would become more difficult if visa program was eliminated.

Mr. KEATING. Okay. Mr. Chairman, my time is up. I yield back.

Mr. KING. The gentleman yields back. I have one question I would like to pursue. Dr. Gartenstein-Ross, in your testimony you mentioned the perhaps greater threat if Syrian refugees do come in of those who are vetted but yet have family members, children perhaps, who become radicalized after they are here.

I would like to ask Mr. Fuentes first: Is it possible; what is the practicality of the FBI surveilling, maintaining a surveillance of Syrian refugees when they come in? Would that violate FBI procedures? Are there sufficient resources to do it? Could it be effective? Then I will ask the other two witnesses for their comments on that.

Mr. FUENTES. I think the answer would be no to all of that. I think the policy of just following people for the sake of it doesn't exist. There has to be some predication that there has been information received or some indication that they are either involved in criminal activity or some activity that threatens National security.

The fact is that when you look at the number of instances that come up that you and I have both been on CNN talking about, is this an intelligence failure? When you have over 1 million names on the TIDE list for example, and a few thousand FBI agents and analysts, there is going to be no way to keep track of that. We hear this over and over. Well, at one time this person was on the FBI's radar. Well, a million people are on the FBI's radar unfortunately. So you really have to have that narrowed down with some degree of specificity and predication before you can actually initiate it.

Now, right now the FBI, as Director Comey has mentioned, they have active counterterrorism investigations in every single State. Then when you take some locations, if that is just one per State minimum, let's say New York, let's say in Chicago, in the District of Columbia, those could be in the dozens; they could be in the hundreds, with that many more number of subjects.

So you could be looking at tens of thousands of potential subjects that there is a reason to follow them but it can't be done, not in every case. They have to prioritize. They have to triage who they are looking at and how many resources are devoted to it. So the practicality in a refugee vetting process, I think just doesn't exist.

Mr. KING. Dr. Gartenstein-Ross, based on what Mr. Fuentes just said, do you see any answer to the question that you raised about the threat of radicalization of those who come to the country?

Mr. GARTENSTEIN-ROSS. I think it is a community for which you would have an elevated level of risk in that regard. I mean, there is a standard narrative in a group like Jabhat al-Nusrah could use, and the reason I focus on al-Nusrah is because I think the Islamic State would actually have more trouble recruiting in this population. It wouldn't be impossible, but it would have a bit more trouble because they understand what the Islamic State has done. It is much more overtly brutal.

Nusrah in contrast is brutal, but it doesn't, you know, tweet out photos of people they have beheaded recently. They don't release videos of them drowning people in a cage in a swimming pool. They also, unlike the Islamic State, work very well with other groups at a local level. So in that regard, the risk would be there as I stated it. The area where I think in the future we can reduce risks is in terms of vetting people as they come in because that is one of the significant questions that has been raised. I should point out that our vetting system is very antiquated. You know, when we are talking about what we look for, what we look for, has Acunia come up? Is their name in a database?

One thing that we should think about is the world is moving towards a big data solution for intelligence across the board. It is not always the solution to everything. There are downsides to big data, but we haven't thought about it in this context. Now, let me say I do work, you know, on this from both sides. I am a security studies person. I also do work on asylum cases for asylees as an expert witness, often pro bono. I talk about country conditions in places like Somalia or Afghanistan.

One of the things that is disturbing about our asylum process is it is really hard to determine if someone is lying. You have their story, and when I am an expert witness, I am not there to say if they are telling the truth. I am just there to say, does their story match with what we know about the country? Now, when we talk about the big data approach, what we don't have, if someone says okay I was in Somalia, I was in Mogadishu in September 2010, and my family was massacred by Shabaab. Well, did that happen?

What I think we should start to move towards is a situation where we take sig acts, significant acts, from these theaters and put them in a database that can be cross-checked in multiple ways so we can see, does their story actually match with what was going on on the ground at that particular time at a granular level?

No. 2, when you look at where they were coming from, do they match with people who were known as militants? Right now we don't have the sort of system in place where you can actually start to get a chance of getting at clean skins or getting at people who there might be some corroborating evidence or some evidence that would tend to refute their story or show that they pose a risk.

That is something we should figure out for the future because this will not be the last refugee crisis that we face, and getting better at our screening will make us safer as a Nation.

Mr. KING. Dr. Jones.

Mr. JONES. Very briefly, on your first FBI question having served last year on the FBI Director's 9/11 Commission and looking at FBI resources now, I mean I strongly agree with Mr. Fuentes' comment, especially when you add the rise in social media use by these groups, the cyber attacks, et cetera. It would not be good for U.S. freedom to be following people without prior indications that they were involved in terrorism.

But I would also note, just to complicate this a little bit, that based on past individuals that have been plotting or have attacked in the United States, it is not clear to me that refugees are more likely to radicalize than others. We have lots of people in the United States that are not refugees that have radicalized, that have converted. So, you know, the problem is clearly much bigger than this.

The last thing I would note—and this goes to a question that Mr. Keating noted earlier, too—is I think the more information we have about these individuals, DNA, biometrics, et cetera, the better it will be, including I do think it is worth considering rescreening procedures before they become eligible for permanent resident status, so potentially looking at several layers here.

Mr. KING. I would just conclude by saying that I think we have raised issues today that there are no, in no way any definitive answers for. I heard what Mr. Katko said about we should never allow refugees in if there is a threat of terrorism. I understand that.

On the other hand, from talking to Jordanian officials, and they are our closest ally, if nothing else just for the diplomatic help that it would give Jordan, we have to show we are doing something. Otherwise King Abdullah could be losing some of his support in Jordan, so it is in our National interest, apart from any moral imperative or whatever, that something be done, and we have to find ways to do it, though, where the vetting is increased, I think or vetted.

So with that, I would—does the Ranking Member have any questions?

Mr. HIGGINS. Yes. For context, the United Nations has indicated that of Western nations resettling Syrian refugees, Germany will resettle the largest number, some 30,000; followed by Canada, about 11- or 12,000. According to the State Department, the United States will resettle about 1,000 to 2,000 this year. More in coming years but, this year. That disparity is attributed to what? Less of a rigorous assessment screening process in Germany and Canada versus the United States? Dr. Jones.

Mr. JONES. I don't know what the process is for why Germany any has allowed more and what the policy discussions are; but I will say that when you look at the foreign fighter problem in Europe, including in Germany, that is connected to Syria, the threat in Germany is serious. They have got more people in Syria than we have.

Mr. HIGGINS. Mr. Fuentes.

Mr. FUENTES. I think we as Americans have pretty much been unaware for many years of the nature of the threat in Europe, and particularly al-Qaeda. Back when 9/11 happened, that obviously dominated U.S. news for weeks and months. What most Americans never heard of was that very week, a couple days after 9/11, al-Qaeda was going to blow up the U.S. Embassy in Paris and conduct bombing attacks in the Netherlands and in Belgium at NATO facilities.

Seven European countries were working with the FBI on those al-Qaeda cells at the time and neutralized them, and I think 14 people were arrested, stood trial, were convicted, served jail sentences. One of them that was the coordinator of the Embassy attack in Paris later was released from jail and helped conduct or coordinate the Charlie Hebdo attack. So these are cells that go back more than a decade in those countries, Germany included. You know, this has been on-going, and I think most Americans don't realize the extent of the threat that has already been in Europe all these years and most of the time successfully neutralized but not always.

Mr. GARTENSTEIN-ROSS. When you are asking about the disparities, I think one of the primary things that is at play with respect to Germany is that you have had a large amount of Syrian refugees come into Europe through the central Mediterranean route. It is a route coming in through Libya. In the third quarter of last year, there were over 75,000 refugees, not refugees rather, but irregular migrants who went in through this route.

One of the majority groups, one of the two largest groups for that quarter, was Syrians of whom they are refugees. Now when Syrians get to Europe, you have in international law, a rule against refoulement, that is a rule against returning them to the country that they were forcibly expelled from. So when they are there, something has to be done with them. In part, Europe trying to set a policy for what to do with Syrians who have gotten there through this route I think plays somewhat of a role in terms of why Germany has taken such high numbers.

With respect to Canada, they have kind of a different set of policies and norms with respect to refugee populations than the United States does, but I wouldn't attribute this to there necessarily being worse screening in any of these countries than in the United States.

Mr. HIGGINS. Got it. Thank you very much. The panel has been very helpful, and I yield back, Mr. Chairman.

Mr. KING. I want to thank all the witnesses for their testimony. This has been I think a very illuminating meeting. It certainly brought out information that I think is vital for the record. It has also raised questions that we have address. I would perhaps indulge on you if we could consult with you as we go forward. Any thoughts or advice you have as this matter goes forward, we would greatly appreciate it.

Also the Members of the subcommittee may have some additional questions for you, and we ask you to respond in writing if you would. With that, pursuant to Committee Rule 7(E), the hearing record will be held open for 10 days. Without objection, the subcommittee stands adjourned.

[Whereupon, at 11:25 a.m., the subcommittee was adjourned.]